SANTE UBERTO BARBIERI

Anthology of Poetry and Prose

Anthology of

POETRY
& PROSE

WITH BIOGRAPHICAL NOTES
ABOUT THE AUTHOR

SANTE
UBERTO
BARBIERI

The Upper Room

SANTE UBERTO BARBIERI
Anthology of Poetry and Prose

We want to thank the following publishing houses for permission to reproduce selections from the following works:

EDITORIAL LA AURORA (Buenos Aires)
For: *Peregrinaciones de mi Espíritu, Pétalos y Espinas de mi Sendero, Del Fango a las Estrellas, Entre Olas y Nieves, Hojas al Viento, El Sacrificio Vivo, La Supereminencia de Jesús, Ni Señores, ni Esclavos, El Médico Amado, Spiritual Currents in Spanish America.*

EDITORIAL EL CAMINO (Buenos Aires)
For: *Una Extraña Estirpe de Audaces*

CUPSA—CASA UNIDA DE PUBLICACIONES, S.A. (México)
For: *El Desafío de la Comunicación del Evangelio, Llamarás su Nombre Jesús, Gotas de Rocío*

EDICIONES ESCRIBE (México)
For: *Cantos de Inquietud y Esperanza*

PUBLICACIONES ALFALIT INTERNACIONAL (San José, Costa Rica)
For: *Meditaciones Poéticas* (First Edition 1981)

METHOPRESS (Buenos Aires)
For: *El Verbo de la Gracia, La Exaltación del Verbo Hecho Carne, Coloquios Intimos*

IMPRENSA METODISTA (São Paulo)
For: *Meditações do Meu Caminho, A Exaltação Do Verbo Feito Carne*

EDITORIAL CLUB DE POETAS (Buenos Aires)
For: *Antología del Anuario de Poetas Contemporáneos*

JUNTA GERAL DE AÇÃO SOCIAL DA IGREJA METODISTA DO BRASIL (São Paulo)
For: *A Ação Social Da Igreja*

CONFEDERAÇAO EVANGELICA DO BRASIL (São Paulo)
For: *Os Ensinos de Jesús*

Book Design: Harriette Bateman

First Printing: March 1983 (5)
Library of Congress Catalog Card Number: 82–70400
ISBN: 0–8358–0441–0
Printed in the United States of America

Contents

Preface   9

MAXIE D. DUNNAM

1. **Barbieri, A Hero of the Faith in Latin America**   11

    GONZALO BÁEZ-CAMARGO

2. **Bishop Sante Uberto Barbieri**
    —The World Is His Parish   23

    J. EARL MORELAND

3. **Poetry**   31

    Beyond   31

    Little One Along My Way   35

    What Troubles Me   37

    I Would Like to Have Those Hands   38

    I Had Never Liked the Pepper Tree   46

    Together   47

Stay With Us   48

Enchanted Night   54

If You Have a Word of Encouragement   58

When Your Life Seems Burdened   61

And the Word Became Flesh   62

Cactus Flower   63

Listening to the Sea   64

Kindness   66

Look at the Birds of the Air   68

Make Love Your Aim   71

Flowers of Sacrifice   73

Insuperable Love   74

Sublimity   75

An Encounter   78

Martin Luther King   81

Anguish   84

While Night Comes . . .   88

Sons of Dust?   93

Blessed Christ!   96

Have Faith in God   98

My Old Age   100

4. **Prose**   101

The Social Action of the Church
The Boundaries of Religion   101

The Teachings of Jesus
Chapter IX: The Family   104

The Teachings of Jesus
Chapter X: The State   105

Wanderings of My Spirit
    Sunflowers   108
    How Much Value Has a Human Being?   111

The Supereminence of Jesus
The Superiority of Jesus over Moses   114

Meditations of My Path
In the Shade of the Eucalyptus Trees   117

Neither Lords Nor Slaves
Act II, Scene I   119

Spiritual Currents in Spanish America
The Spirit of the Spanish Conquest   124

Who Leads You?
To the Young People of the Church   128

A Strange Lineage of Daring People
    Stories of Methodist Pioneers: Introduction   129
    Chapter VIII: The One Who Wished to Have the
        Wings of an Eagle   130

The Beloved Physician   132

You Shall Call His Name Jesus
Chapter VI: World Citizen   138

The Challenge of the Communication of the Gospel
The Unavoidable Mission of Christians   140

The Woman with Christ   147

Preface

PERHAPS more than any other person in this century, in Latin America, especially among Protestants, Bishop Sante Uberto Barbieri, through his writings, his preaching, and his pastoral leadership, has provided devotional inspiration and has cultivated Christian spirituality.

This anthology, which is being published on the occasion of the presentation of the *1982 Upper Room Citation,* to Bishop Barbieri, is representative of his own spiritual and literary journey.

In being so honored, Bishop Barbieri joins a gallery of renowned Christians—John R. Mott, Frank Laubach, Gonzalo Báez-Camargo, Margaret T. Applegarth, Rita Snowden, Billy Graham, and others who have been recipients of this signal recognition.

The recipients of this Citation are persons who demonstrate in their own life the meaning of devotional living. In selecting these persons, special attention is given to their contributions and accomplishments in the following areas:

- Assisting other people in an understanding and practice of prayer.
- Writing devotional resources.
- Cultivating spirituality through their life and ministry.
- Developing programs of spiritual renewal.

- Providing research in the area of spiritual formation.

It is with great joy and excitement that we present this volume of his writings and with sincere and deep appreciation for his life and ministry that we present to him the *1982 Upper Room Citation*.

Maxie D. Dunnam
WORLD EDITOR
THE UPPER ROOM

1.

Barbieri, A Hero of the Faith in Latin America

FOR MANY of those who attended, in the summer of 1952, the Conference of the International Missionary Council in Willingen, Germany, the person in charge of the daily devotionals and Bible studies was not as well known as he deserved to be. Dr. Sante Uberto Barbieri came from Argentina, and this was his first formal contact with the ecumenical movement. He was already, however, a very distinguished figure in Latin American Protestantism—Bishop, since 1949, of the Methodist Church for the River Plate region, Uruguay, and Bolivia.

The first thing in his Bible studies at Willingen which attracted his audience's attention was the way he read the Scriptures. He read, not with the traditional and monotonous semi-chant, but with freshness, clarity and modulation. His voice was warm and sonorous. "Never had I heard the Bible read like that," said a lady who heard him the first day. "It seemed to me that I was listening to poetry."

But even before he had finished his series of Bible studies, everybody was aware that there was much more in them than a new, beautiful way of reading the Scriptures. There was depth and at the same time clarity, sound exegesis and an inspired message, sincere devotion and an innermost human warmth. Through his quiet exposition of the Word one could perceive his rich, mature experience as a pastor, teacher, evangelist, theologian, poet and ecumenist.

Background

Sante Uberto Barbieri was born in 1902 in Dueville, a town in the province of Vicenza, Italy. He was only about nine years old when the family—his father and mother and he—emigrated to Brazil. They settled in São Paulo, where his father engaged in commerce and Sante attended school, soon becoming conversant in Portuguese. He was a devoted and brilliant student. Not satisfied with what he learned in the classroom, he was a voracious reader and very soon could also read French and Spanish.

He, nevertheless, was finally forced to suspend his studies at school when his father fell ill. His father's health became progressively worse and he was unable to look after his business. Only sixteen, Sante had to take over. It was very hard work and he had to travel a good deal, generally on horseback, for great distances. With his merchandise he also carried many books which he read at his mount's ambling, in the saddle, and at the inns in the evenings, robbing himself of many hours of sleep.

The family had been moving from one place to another. From São Paulo they moved to Caxias, in the state of Rio Grande do Sul, and then to Passo Fundo. In this city, when Sante was 20, his father died. With his widowed mother, an energetic and courageous woman, the young man had to face the new situation and to assume full responsibility for the family. But business was not his real vocation. He became a writer and journalist. He began contributing to the only newspaper in town, and he also lectured. He had not yet found, however, the road he would finally follow.

The Methodist

It was as a journalist that he made his first contact with the Methodists. There were a church and a school of this denomination in Passo Fundo. One day Sante found a leaflet that had been discarded on the street and as one who used to read everything he happened to have at hand, he picked it up and read it. It had been written by a Roman Catholic priest and contained a bitter attack on the Methodists. Sante's father, a strong liberal, had brought

12

him up as an ardent lover of freedom of conscience. The contents of the pamphlet provoked such strong indignation in him that he decided to take up in the newspaper the defense of the Methodists' right to profess and practice their beliefs, although at the time he did not even know what these beliefs were.

He signed his article as Livio di Sante Uberto. Its publication raised quite a storm. There were some people who jumped to the priest's defense. Others sided with Sante Uberto, although they could not identify the writer right away. The Methodist pastor, Reverend Daniel L. Betts, looked him up and paid him a visit in order to thank him for his defense. He came to know then that Sante had had to suspend his studies and invited him to continue them in the Methodist College, and also to teach there. Sante accepted, and thus began a closer acquaintance with the Methodists.

Two incidents led the young man to finally embrace the Christian faith in the sheepfold of Methodism. The first was Rev. Betts' pastoral call when Sante's father was near death. The pastor read from the scriptures and prayed at his bedside. When he finished, the old man was quietly crying. After Reverend Betts departed, he said to his son: "Those were the very words I needed at this precise moment. Had I followed that religion in my youth, I would have been a different kind of man."

Sante meditated on his father's words for a long time. Soon after the old man died, Sante wanted to know "that religion" better; so he began to attend the Methodist services regularly. The second incident occurred almost eight months later. Reverend Betts, who had noticed both the interest and the indecision of the young man, one day took him aside, talked to him about Christ and his personal love for him, and invited Sante to follow Him. "He put his right arm upon my shoulder," wrote Sante himself, "while he waited for my answer. Breaking the silence that followed, I answered him firmly, 'Yes, I will follow him.' "

A week later, on Easter Sunday, Sante and his mother were received as members of the Methodist Church. And after five months, Sante joined the Methodist ministry on probation in the Southern Annual Conference of Brazil.

Sante Uberto Barbieri was to become one of the outstanding Methodists, not only of Latin America but of the world at large. After serving in several capacities, first in Brazil, then in the River Plate region, he was elected Bishop in 1949. Reelected again and again, he filled that high position for 21 years. He then became the Executive Secretary of the Latin American Council of Methodist Churches.

The Pastor

The life and work of Sante Uberto Barbieri as a Christian worker is marked, above all, with a pastoral zeal. He is at heart, first and foremost, a pastor. In this he is assisted by his personable, simple, kind manner, always full of human warmth, imparting friendliness and understanding. He inspires trust at first sight. Without resorting to sanctimonious commonplaces, without feigning any show of fervor, his word is impregnated with a deep faith and a genuine religious experience.

While finishing his ministerial training in the Theological Seminary in Porto Alegre, he began his pastoral work in the Gloria Mission with a congregation of eight members. Later, he would become a pastor in Cachoeira. In constant ascension he would, as the years passed, occupy in succession the pastorates of Porto Alegre, Passo Fundo and Buenos Aires (Central Church).

Once in his episcopate, he would become a veritable shepherd of shepherds. More than a superior, the pastors in his jurisdiction in Argentina, Uruguay and Bolivia, found in him a friend, a colleague, an elder brother, a wise and affectionate counselor, not only in personal matters but also in pastoral affairs. Indeed, many of the pastors who served in the episcopal area under his direction will be ready to subscribe to what one of them wrote to him, ''I feel I must write these lines in order to express to you my personal gratitude for all you have meant in my ministry.''

The Teacher

Already we have seen the extraordinary circumstances in which Sante Uberto Barbieri began his career as a Methodist teacher. With his pastoral vocation he received his vocation as a teacher. He was at the same time the pastor of the Central Methodist Church in Porto Alegre and the Dean of the Southern Theological Seminary. From his four years of postgraduate studies in the United States (to which we shall refer presently), he had returned with a broad vision of what theological studies ought to be. But at the time, the Methodist Church of Brazil was going through a crisis, which affected its program of ministerial education. As a consequence, Barbieri could not carry out his plans for the seminary.

This situation, however, did not put an end to his career as a teacher. He had been asked several times to speak at different meetings of the River Plate region and thus had established relations with the Methodists in that area. Finally, they were so favorably impressed by the Brazilian teacher's personality, qualifications, and training, that they encouraged him to settle and work among them. So in 1940, he was transferred to the River Plate Region Annual Conference. He was appointed a Professor in the School of Theology, of which he would later become Dean in 1948, and pastor of the Barracas Circuit.

His work as a teacher opened up new horizons. Both in the classroom and in his role as supervisor of the pastoral students' practice, he had the opportunity to apply his ideas about theological education, which he had had no chance to put into practice in Brazil. As a teacher he influenced the formation of a generation of distinguished South American ministers. Combining his teaching with his pastoral work, he was a teacher to his congregations, and a friend, a counselor, and, in fact, a pastor, to his students.

The Evangelist

From the early years of his initiation in the ministry, Barbieri put a definite evangelistic emphasis upon his preaching and his pastoral work. His personal encounter with Christ had brought about a profound transformation in him and had given new meaning and direction to his life. For this reason his unceasing endeavor was to guide others to meet the Lord and Savior, and to follow Him with the firm determination with which he had followed Him.

However, anyone who may try to find in Barbieri the conventional image of the "evangelist" will be disappointed. Through his powerful and indeed evangelical preaching, he could have made a famous professional evangelist of himself, although the power of his messages does not lie in the eloquence of a brilliant orator nor in an appeal to mere emotion. His word is calm, but persuasive. He touches the heart but at the same time makes people think.

Because of his earnest interest in evangelization, the Methodist Church of Argentina appointed him Executive Secretary for Evangelism in 1947. He discharged this function until his election as bishop in 1949. But from his new position he never ceased to impart to the pastors in his jurisdiction the evangelistic spirit, both with his counsel and his example.

The Theologian

For a preacher and teacher like Barbieri, faithful to the Wesleyan spirit, theology is an inner nourishment, not a dogmatic obsession. It might, therefore, seem out of order to single out from among his wealth of talents that of theologian. He is not fond of the dry postulates of dogmatic theology, but his sermons and writings are permeated with a clear and sound biblical and evangelical theology.

Theology is to them what the skeleton is to the human body. It does not show itself, because that would be a sure sign of starvation. But it is there underneath, as the support that keeps it erect and firm, and that enables it to engage in vigorous activity. From 1933 to 1939 he widened and rounded the theological preparation in the Porto Alegre Theological School, where he had obtained the degree of Licentiature in Theology, with postgraduate studies at Southern Methodist University and Emory University in the United States.

At SMU he earned a B.A. in philosophy, a B.D. in Church

History, and a master's degree in the Old Testament, which included Hebrew. At Emory he graduated with a master's degree in the New Testament. His thesis on "The nature and relationship of faith and love in St. Paul" established him, as much for the choice as the treatment of the subject, as a biblical theologian rather than a systematic one. This has been confirmed by the numerous devotional meditations, sermons, lectures, articles and books, in which he has shown fruitful activity that has covered many countries and several continents. The strength of his theological thought is revealed in such lectureships as the "Elizabeth M. Lee" series (Cuba, 1950) on "Man and His World," the Fondren Lectures (SMU, Dallas), and those given at Randolph-Macon College (Ashland, Virginia) on "Spiritual Currents in Hispanic America."

The same theological theme may be found in his books *The Teachings of Jesus, The Teacher of Galilee, The Lord's Prayer, The Supereminence of Jesus, The Exaltation of the Word Made Flesh,* and others, most of which have also appeared in Portuguese.

The Writer

As we have already seen, from his early youth Sante Uberto Barbieri experienced the vocation of writer. The prodigious amount of literature he assimilated, which enriched his spirit, gave rise in him to a powerful impulse to express himself both orally and in writing. For that reason he began as a journalist. But the newspaper pages, so relatively ephemeral, did not satisfy him as a vehicle for his thoughts. More and more ideas surfaced which required more extension and depth than that which the development of an article allowed.

After joining Methodism, he went on writing articles and essays, now mainly for Protestant publications. His signature appears frequently in them, not only in Methodist publications but in those of other denominations as well. From 1943 to 1967 he was the editor of a journal for preachers—*El Predicador Evangélico.* A man of three worlds, he has written articles not only in Spanish but also in English and Portuguese. Many of his devotional writings have appeared in *The Upper Room*.

He was, however, intensely attracted to the book as a wider and more permanent means of expression. His first book, *Estevão* (Stephen), in Portuguese, appeared in 1929 when he was the pastor of the church in Cachoeira, Brazil. This novel about the first Christian martyr was the beginning of a rich bibliography: biblical novels, didactic works, poetry, theological and moral treatises, devotional meditations, biographies, plays, history of missions, biblical commentaries, social essays. There is almost no literary genre in which Barbieri has not produced mature works. His Spanish and Portuguese bibliography at present reaches almost forty titles and at least two have been published in English and another one in Italian.

His literary pursuits have not been limited to religious circles. In 1938 he founded in Passo Fundo, Brazil, the Passo Fundo Guild of Letters, now an Academy. He had previously participated in the First Congress of Academies of Letters and Societies for Literary Culture, held in Rio de Janeiro in 1936. There he submitted a paper on ''Shepherds' Poetry.'' In 1939, in the same city, when the Second Congress met, he presented a paper on ''The Literacy Program for the Proletarian Masses.'' He is an elected lifetime member of the Rio Grande Academy of Letters.

Barbieri's style is delicate, simple, clear, and carefully composed. Although Spanish is not his mother tongue, he has come to handle it with great ease, accuracy, mastery, and force. He was brought up in Brazil, with Italian as his first language and Portuguese as his second, and spent most of his life as a resident and citizen of Argentina. Nevertheless, his Spanish is free of Italianisms, Portuguesisms and Argentinian regionalisms that might obscure it. Considering his background, this is something that those of us who are zealous defenders of the integrity of the Spanish language appreciate and for which we are very grateful to him.

The Poet

Barbieri's gentle and sensitive character, at times perhaps a bit introverted, or at least discreet and retiring, clearly shows that the vocation of poetry is fundamental in him. It is perhaps in his poems that the rich stream of his inner life overflows and is best expressed. His sermons, lectures and writings, no matter what the subject, always have a poetic flair to them so that even his prose becomes beautiful and musical.

Barbieri possesses a fine poetic insight, an almost permanent state of wonder and love about the world around him. He finds inspiration for his poetry in many things that are overlooked by the average, unimaginative, materialistic person. A stone, a flower, the leaf carried by the wind, the landscape that unfolds before his eyes, all nature, the work of the God in whom he believes and whom he loves, inspire him with thoughts and emotions that he pours into his poems.

And in the human sphere, for every being, from the vagrant boy and the passing stranger, to the friend and his brother in the faith, or his family and relatives, for all of them he feels sympathy, understanding and affection which he expresses in his poems. His Christian faith is revealed in religious compositions of high quality and extraordinary depth.

Fourteen of his books are poetry, which he modestly prefers to call "poetic prose" because he has not adopted strict meter and rhyme according to classical rules, but the kind of verse which is called in Spanish "blank"or "free." It certainly seems easier, but it is actually more difficult, for without precise measure and rhyme, it has to depend exclusively on the sense of rhythm, that is to say, on the music that results from the natural sound of words and the cadence which is produced by their order.

Sante Uberto Barbieri is one of the greatest Protestant poets in Latin America.

The Ecumenist

Along the paths of Methodism, Sante Uberto Barbieri had his personal encounter with Christ. In the fold of Methodism, he found his spiritual home and has occupied its highest position, but this fact has not made him a sectarian. Indeed, right from the very first moment he captured and has been true to the broad spirit of Methodism, for which the strongest convictions of conscience are in no way in conflict with an appreciation of the richness of the doctrines and practices of other Christian bodies or with the concept of brotherly love for all believers in Christ.

This has led him to cooperate with other denominations in several Latin American countries, both in teaching and preaching, and also to participate in national and international ecumenical conferences. In world ecumenical organizations he has been given important positions of leadership and in all his activities in that field, Barbieri has been a worthy representative of Latin American Protestantism, a living example of the positive results of the missionary enterprise in our lands.

In 1949 he was elected Chairman of the First Latin American Conference of Evangelical [Protestant] Churches, meeting in Buenos Aires. He, then, in 1952, acted as chaplain at the Willingen meeting of the International Missionary Council. Following that, in 1954 he attended the Assembly of the World Council of Churches in Evanston, Illinois, where he was elected one of the six Presidents of that organization, a position he occupied until 1961, when the next Assembly of the Council took place at New Delhi, and a new roster of Presidents was elected. But, as a token of the great appreciation he had won for himself in the Council, he was appointed to the Executive Committee and the Central Committee of the Council. In this capacity he participated in the Uppsala (Sweden) Assembly in 1968.

The World Council of Christian Education was another ecumenical body in whose activities he shared and in which he also had a high position. He attended the Council's Assembly in Tokyo, in 1958, and was appointed there as one of the vice-chairmen, a position he held until 1970, when the WCCE merged with the WCC.

Bishop Barbieri has been the recipient of many well deserved honors and distinctions. He has been a Doctor of Laws, *honoris causa*, of Southern Methodist University, and Doctor in Human

Letters, also *honoris causa*, of Emory University since 1956. He also holds the SMU Diploma of Distinguished Alumnus. He was a member in 1970–71 of *The National Register of Prominent American and International Notables*, Venice, Florida. The Government of Bolivia honored him in 1968 with that country's highest decoration for a foreigner—a Knight of the Order of the Condor of the Andes.

All that has been said is only a brief sketch of the person and work of Sante Uberto Barbieri; there is still much more to say. In publishing the present Anthology, *The Upper Room* adds its homage of admiration and recognition to one of the greatest heroes of the faith in Latin America.

GONZALO BÁEZ-CAMARGO
MEXICO

2.

Bishop Sante Uberto Barbieri
— The World Is His Parish

MEET the brilliant young defender of freedom in Passo Fundo!

It was October, 1921. That was my introduction to Sante Uberto Barbieri, an introduction made by Snr. Pindaro Annes, lay leader in the Methodist Church, industrialist and writer. "You two," he added, "ought to become friends." We did become friends, and the friendship has lasted through sixty years.

Barbieri was only nineteen years of age at the time, but had already become well known in Passo Fundo and the surrounding area through his articles in defense of freedom. In a thoughtful, well-written, persuasive thesis, he had made his point that freedom was a birthright in free Brazil. Handsome and impressive in appearance, with the ability to think clearly and to express his thoughts, he brought people to assess their positions on basic principles of citizenship. He also challenged the authoritarians of the established church. As the days passed, his well publicized beliefs and arguments appealed more and more clearly to a large body of citizens. Freedom of religion, freedom of the faith, came to be accepted principles, basic beliefs. The articles eventually came to an end, but the ideas remained.

Sante's father was a man who held tenaciously to his philosophy of life. That philosophy began and ended with strong opposition to oppression and dictatorship in any and all forms. When he was seventeen he went to Switzerland from Dueville, Italy, in search of work. In Switzerland he met a young woman, María

Luisa Zanzotto, whom he married. Their first child was born near Zurich. About two years later he left Switzerland to go to the United States, but his wife went to Dueville, where the second child, Sante Uberto, was born. When Sante Uberto was six months old, she left him with her mother-in-law and went with the first child to meet her husband in New York. There they remained until 1908, when they went back to Italy alone. Their first child and a third child born in the United States had died. They took Sante Uberto with them and went back to Switzerland, then to Germany, and again back to Switzerland.

In 1910 Sante's father went to Brazil alone. On his way, the boat stopped in Lisbon, Portugal, when an uprising was going on. He left the boat and took part in the revolution, for which an honorary citizenship was bestowed on him. In 1911, Sante Barbieri and his mother moved to São Paulo, where they lived till 1915. They then went to Caxias and, after some years, to Passo Fundo, where Sante's father died in 1922.

Under the guidance and influence of Reverend Daniel L. Betts, pastor of the Methodist Church in Passo Fundo, the young defender of a free way of life came to study the Bible. As he began to understand that a new way of life was offered, his whole life underwent a profound change. He saw clearly that Christ and his church opened the door to happiness and fulfillment. He joined the Methodist Church. As the days passed, Barbieri felt that Jesus Christ was calling him to enter the ministry, and he accepted the call. Enrolling in the local Methodist College (Instituto Ginasial) to continue his studies, he took a class in English which I taught. His first assignment was planned to cover work for the entire semester, but after three weeks he reported that he was ready for the final examination. His grade? 100.

Barbieri became interested in a gifted young lady, Dona Odette de Oliveira, Professor of Portuguese in the college. The interest led to a commitment, and they were married in 1924. They left after their marriage for Porto Alegre, capital of the state of Rio Grande do Sul and home of Porto Alegre College. Barbieri became a student there, while serving his first appointment as pastor of Gloria Mission, taking courses in both the undergraduate school and the School of Theology. He was profoundly influenced by Dean James M. Terrell, a graduate of the Vanderbilt School of Religion, who gave scholarly direction to Barbieri's study and reinforced his commitment to a life of learning and to scholarly attainments. At commencement in 1926, he was awarded the degree of Bacharel de Teologia, as the first graduate of Porto Alegre College.

Assigned, after graduation, to the Methodist Church in Cachoeira, one of south Brazil's stronger churches, Barbieri still hungered. He came for a visit with me one year later, and informed me of his decision to undertake further study.

"I must learn more!," he said. "The books are not available for the work I must find and carry out. I want to go to your country, where university study is readily available." I recommended my alma mater, Southern Methodist University in Dallas, Texas, and the way was found for Barbieri and his family to go to the United States. After three years of intensive study, he came to commencement to be awarded three degrees: Bachelor of Arts, Master of Arts, and Bachelor of Divinity. He stayed one more year in the United States, to study at Emory University and receive from that institution the degree of Master of Arts with honors. His first appointment, on returning to Brazil, was to Central Methodist Church in Porto Alegre, the largest church in the South Brazil Annual Conference. Shortly thereafter, he accepted appointment as Dean of the School of Theology at his "first" alma mater. It was during this time that Barbieri was invited to give lectures in New Testament before the Union Theological Seminary in Buenos Aires, where young ministers were trained for churches in the Spanish-speaking countries of South America. He accepted appointment as professor, and in 1947 he was appointed dean. At the Central Conference held a bit later, he was elected Bishop of the Methodist Church in the River Plate and Bolivia areas, which served the countries of Argentina, Uruguay and Bolivia. The assignment entailed constant travel, continued preaching and lecturing, and providing leadership for the churches in the area. It was a significant post, and one which Barbieri served for twenty-one years.

During those years, he continued without interruption his study, the writing of books, and lecturing at colleges and seminaries. The ability to write and speak four languages enabled him to publish the books and serve a wide constituency; Portuguese, Spanish, Italian, and English were familiar to him and spoken fluently.

When he went to Bolivia to preside over the last annual conference before his retirement, Barbieri was surprised to find that the President of Bolivia had flown over the mountain in that mountainous country to present personally Bolivia's highest award given to a foreigner, "El cóndor de los Andes."

It was only one of a long list of honors that have come to my distinguished friend. Bishop Barbieri's accomplishments and awards are so numerous that I must present them in outline form, certain as I am that the list will be incomplete. (He is 7,000 miles south of my Virginia home, and the publisher more than 700 miles to the west as I write!)

He was elected to membership in The Academy of Letters of South Brazil, the highest honor which can be given a writer in that area. The founder of "O Gremio Passofundense de Letras," in the growing city of Passo Fundo on south Brazil's beautiful mountain ranges, his contribution toward stimulating and promoting the interests of promising young writers was significant from that moment. It continues to this day.

In 1951, Southern Methodist University chose Barbieri as Distinguished Alumnus of the Year. This recognition and honor is reserved for those alumni who have made "signal contributions" to their country and their alma mater. Few such honors are awarded, and for an alumnus from abroad it is indeed rare!

Another year, 1956, the Bishop was also singularly honored in the United States. Southern Methodist University conferred on him the honorary degree of "Doctor of Laws," and Emory University awarded the honorary degree of "Doctor of Humanities." It is indeed a rare event in the history of American higher education for two of America's foremost universities to honor one man in the same year.

On February 24, 1973, the Methodist Hospital in La Paz, Bolivia, inaugurated a new hall, dedicated to pediatrics, and they named it Sante Uberto Barbieri Hall.

He was invited, in 1950, to give the Alexander G. Brown Lectures at Randolph-Macon College, and in the same year he gave the Fondren Lectures at his "second" alma mater, Southern Methodist University, on the subject of "Spiritual Currents in Latin America."

Barbieri served from 1970 to 1978 as Executive Secretary of the Council of Methodist Churches in Latin America. The timeliness and values of his labors in this area included an emphasis on the necessity of stressing the ecumencial movement—worldwide. During the past half-century this movement has gained attention and interest from churches in many lands. The urgency of its implementation in the countries of Central and South America is vital to the growth and progress of the Protestant churches, and Barbieri's contributions to the movement through studies and addresses have been immeasurable.

Barbieri was elected a delegate, representing the Methodist Churches in Spanish America, to the Second General Assembly of the World Council of Churches at Northwestern University in Evanston, Illinois. My service as a member of that assembly included chairmanship of the nominating committee. It was this committee's responsibility to choose the ninety members of the Central Committee—and to choose and present to the assembly nomination of the six members of the Presidium. I presented Barbieri's name, indicating to my five fellow committee members that no representative of Central or South America had been recognized through selection to a high position in the council. After the committee agreed, and in line with written orders of the assembly, I interviewed personally each of the six men for the Presidium. When I visited with Barbieri, and informed him of the nomination, he bowed his head and said, "My friend of the long years, do you really think I am qualified to serve in this high

27

position?'' I replied that I had never been more certain of anything in my life. With head still bowed, he said, "Então, si Deus quizer, eu aceitarei a nomeção"—"If God wills, I will accept the nomination." The humble spirit of the man was never more in evidence.

Bishop Barbieri was a member of the Central Committee of the World Council of Churches from 1954 until 1968. This committee is charged with the responsibility of overseeing the work of the Council between meetings of the General Assembly, and involves extensive travel both before and after meetings. The importance of interpreting the decisions arrived at to the churches in many lands is not easily overstated.

One instance may serve to illustrate, in a small measure, what he has meant to the World Council of Churches. At the Third General Assembly of the World Council held in New Delhi, India, he was distinguished in his efforts as a member of the presidium. On the evening when the Archbishop of Canterbury was the speaker, fellow members of the Presidium chose Barbieri to introduce the Archbishop. At the end of the evening, the leader of the British Methodist delegation came to me and remarked, "I was far more impressed and inspired by the presiding of your friend than by the Archbishop's speech!"

My friend's wife, Dona Odette de Oliveira Barbieri, and her sister, Dona Otilia de Oliveira Chaves, have also made enormous contributions to the church. Dona Otilia served one term as President of the International Federation of Methodist Women and also taught a course in missions at Scarritt College in Nashville, Tennessee. Both have utilized their knowledge and abilities to preside over their homes and family life and the rearing of their children. This service can be recognized as the more remarkable when it is remembered that, in both families, there has been constant travel and service in many areas. Dona Otilia's husband, Reverend Derly de Azevedo Chaves, was asked to write a brief life of Bishop Barbieri when the latter completed fifty years of faithful service. To all who read Portuguese, I heartily recommend this excellent biography.

Books written by the Bishop cover many areas of study and

interest. Mention is made here of those books which my friend sent to me across the years—three books of New Testament studies, two books of poetry in Portuguese, two books of poetry in Spanish, two books of poetry in English, and many devotional studies. His friends had a saying that "Ele está sempre com o livro na mão"—"He always has a book in his hand!"

Now officially retired, Bishop Barbieri continues his travels, his preaching and lectures—and his writing of books. In 1979, he lectured and preached in churches in the North Central Jurisdiction and also in the Southeastern Jurisdiction, he made a return visit to the campus of Randolph-Macon College, where he lectured and gave interviews.

Two quotations are appropriate here. These were Barbieri's closing words, as he completed the Fondren Lectures at Southern Methodist University:

> The Christian Gospel is an inheritance for the whole world. It does not belong to this group or that group. It belongs to humanity as a whole. And none of us who march toward the conquest of the world in God's name should be recognized by any other sign than the spirit of Him who, for love of His fellow men, gave His life on the barren arms of the cross.

When he came to retirement, the Bishop left this message for the people:

> I do not feel a stranger in any country. We are all God's people, and He knows no geographical limits. We all march toward the goal of life eternal.

Barbieri, my friend, has followed faithfully in the path and mission of John Wesley: "The world is his parish!"

J. EARL MORELAND

3.

Poetry

Beyond

Shall I write *The End*
to these my pilgrimages?
The End?
No!
My wanderings do not end here,
they are starting.
The End?
No!
There is still a beyond.

My spirit will continue to wander,
beyond that path,
beyond that star,
beyond that dream,
always beyond.

I detest the alley without exit
which ends at the high impenetrable wall.
I shun the cisterns' stagnant waters
that do not murmur, sing nor move along.
I abhor the words without hope:
never,

impossible,
it is finished,
the end.
They speak of nights without dawn,
of death without an awakening,
of winter without a spring
and are silent about the beyond.

I love the water coming down from the mountain,
playful, musical,
losing itself far away
among the weeds;
like the dreamy soul
looking for mysterious
and distant regions. . . .
the beyond.

I love the path which
climbing the slope,
throws itself into space
to explore infinity
like a bold spirit
which refuses to be lost in nothingness,
and wants to breathe the ethereal aura
beyond the stars.
Beyond.

I love the winged thought,
with its eagerness to explore virgin spots,
like a wandering butterfly,
that flies from flower to flower,
from meadow to meadow,
always seeking something not yet found:
a color not yet seen,
a sweetness not yet tasted,
coming
and going,
zigzagging to and fro,

and going up and down,
and finally losing itself in the horizon.
In the beyond.

No, I will not be limited
by the achievements of yesterday,
nor those of today,
I will think of those of tomorrow.

Yes, tomorrow, the dawn will smile
more sweetly
more beautifully,
full of enchantments.

Yes, tomorrow the night will have more light,
more perfume,
more serenity.

Yes, tomorrow, the task will be nobler,
more perfect,
more enduring.

Yes, tomorrow, love will be purer,
more sincere,
more genuine.

Yes, tomorrow I will find more unexplored fields,
richer,
more fertile.

Yes, tomorrow the great day
anxiously waited for,
will come,
the great day of the beyond.

Friend,
may you too fall in love with the beyond,
walk the second mile,
do not remain asleep,
with heavy eyes
and a tormented soul,

33

like the fishermen of Galilee
in the garden of Gethsemane.

Instead, like the Master,
go a little farther,
even when the beyond may make you
sweat tears of blood,
hear the sonnet of pain
and drink the cup of gall.

Do not pause,
do not sleep,
do not grow weary
never be defeated:
go ahead, struggle and wait.

Go a little beyond;
the cross will not be the end,
beyond the outstretched arms
beyond the agony,
thirst,
contempt,
the way of the dawn will open,
among the green
and flowers
under the sun,
singing of life.
This path launches you toward infinity
and spurs you to proceed,
always higher,
always farther
always toward *the beyond*.

This is not the end,
here my pilgrimage proceeds
toward the everlasting path of *the beyond*.

Buenos Aires
January 19, 1942

Little One Along My Way

Little one along my way,
I cannot forget your dark eyes.
At the station,
through the windows of the train
they looked at me with sad and steadfast gaze,
the vacant melancholy
of one who for long
has not seen a table set.
No, I cannot forget those dark eyes
that spoke to me while I was eating,
"Mister, why do I have so little
while you have such abundance?"

Little one along my way,
I cannot forget your sad face,
the face of one who lives in this great big world
orphan of love
empty of hope
and lacking in spirit.
That downhearted, dirty face of yours
continues to question me,
"Mister, for children like me
is there nothing but street and wind?"

Little one along my way,
I have not forgotten your tattered clothes,
that coat and trousers in rags
which the wind tried to tear to shreds.

Your bare feet walked on the
cold, damp stones of the platform
on that rainy, foggy day
while I, warm and comfortable,
was eating in the dining car
so perfectly at ease.

Your torn clothing of a beggar child
still tonight is asking me,
"Mister, when will children like me
have enough food, shelter, education, and love?"

Little one along my way,
if you only knew of my eagerness
for the train to leave at once
so I would no longer see your sad look
and your pale face and ragged clothes.
I could then finish my meal in peace.
But in vain the train moved on.
Your words of thanks for my small gift
ring harshly in my ear,
"For a hunger as great as mine
why are you giving me so little?"

Little one along my way,
what is your name?
Where did you come from?
In vain I close my eyes
so as not to see your face.
Constantly I see you,
here, there, and everywhere.
You come to meet me, multiplied
into thousands and millions.
In you I see all the children of the earth
who suffer all the misfortunes of poverty,
wandering aimlessly without love.

Through your eyes they all look at me,
under your ragged clothes they all shiver,
through your hand they all beg,
and in your sadness they all groan.
And behind you,
blessing you with a gesture of mercy,
there stands a Man
whose forehead is furrowed with grief
and whose eyes look severely and penetratingly.

He opens His mouth to ask us bitterly,
"Did I not tell you,
indeed many years ago,
that it is not the will of your Heavenly Father
that one of these little ones should perish?"

Santiago, Chile
August 25, 1943

What Troubles Me

It is not my salvation or damnation
that disturbs my spirit;
I want to know if I have lived in vain
or if my life has served for something,
especially for someone.

I want to know if what is left behind me
is straw, ashes, stubble
or deeds that will last through eternity
because of the love and grace of my hands and spirit
among sorrowful souls and aching hearts.

I want to know if I have sown thistles and thorns
or hopes and blessings
along the path of my pilgrimage through this world.

I want to know if the song that has come from my lips
carried anyone to the Mountain of Enchantment
to hear the silence of the starry sky
and the harmony of imperishable things.

I want to know if my countenance and my glance
have inspired a holy enthusiasm,
an ardent zeal, a noble aspiration
in someone who was struggling in the valley of this life.

37

I do not need to know if for me there is
heaven or hell
joy or torment.
I want to know, indeed, that this body
which I touch and this soul which I feel
aflame with unrest
has served, by God's grace
if only for one day
or for just one hour,
to carpet the path of others
with some few petals of fraternal grace
and let fall some drops of heavenly balm
which will soften the bitter wounds
of their daily life.

Buenos Aires
July 5, 1944

I Would Like to Have Those Hands

Softly and melodiously
the notes of the organ
in the small chapel
invaded my soul
that rosy morning
caressed by the golden light of the autumn,
when the leaves from the trees,
one here and one there,
were beginning to fall.
On the communion table,
at the altar,
stood a vase with red roses
roses so red they seemed
to have absorbed all the redness of the dawn.

From the white wall
behind the table
it seemed to me that two hands
were appearing;
those hands took the roses,
and, at the touch of the fingers
their petals fell apart
gently and delicately.
And those white hands
took those red petals
and tossed them gracefully
among those who
were meditating
in silence
in the pews.
I gazed at those hands,
those hands that were scattering roses,
and I saw that they were wounded
and were dripping with blood
as red as the flowers;
hands of Jesus,
hands wounded by the treacherous thorns
of my path and yours;
hands of Jesus
sowing petals of roses
in your path and mine;
hands of Jesus that know anguish
but in their eternal sowing
disseminate
blessing,
  hope,
    love.

And in that mystic hour
on that autumnal morning
I had a warm and deep desire
which went up

with the notes of the organ,
to God's throne:
   "I would like to have those hands:
   Jesus' hands.
   Yes, those hands of his
   I would like to have
   that, having been rocked
   in the cradle of Bethlehem of Judea,
   were wounded with mortal blows
   on the arms of a cross
   on the heights of Golgotha.

   "I would like to have those hands
   which knew how to build
   houses for people
   in that small village of Nazareth.
   I would like to have those hands:
   hands that speak, clamor, and appeal;
   hands that point to heaven
   and want to show us God;
   hands that rest on the troubled soul
   and proclaim resurrection;
   hands that repose on the heart
   and whisper fortitude and peace.

   "I would like to have those hands:
   open hands, and arms, stretched out
   toward the disheartened multitudes,
   flocks abandoned by the careless shepherd,
   those open hands that invite us
   to place on his loving breast
   the anguish, the grief, and the sorrow
   of our heart and soul;
   those open hands that ask,
   with serene grace
   and silent prayer,
   that, like him
   we might be gentle and lowly of heart.

"I would like to have those hands:
hands that broke the bread
in the desert of Galilee of the Gentiles,
for the hungry multitudes;
those hands that also break the bread of eternal life
for the lost souls
in the desert of this world,
bread from the fields and bread from heaven
for your life and mine.

"I would like to have those hands.
hands that reject the proud Pharisaic spirit
and the haughty domineering eye
and the covetous hand gripping gold;
but that caress the restless head
of the child unaware of the dangers of the world
who projects himself toward tomorrow
with smiles on his lips
and joy dancing in his eyes.

"I would like to have those hands:
hands that seek and find the lost sheep
on the steep hillside;
hands that soothe the wound
while they cure it;
hands that lift the lost one
onto his shoulders
to carry it to the safe sheepfold
of the eternal love of God.

"I would like to have those hands:
hands that call boatmen from the still waters,
to go with him
daringly,
to the high seas of the world,
to marvelous and risky fishing
for the kingdom of God;
the kingdom of tranquility and goodwill
that you and I have dreamed of with earnest zeal

41

and so many visionaries have desired
ever since the day when Cain, the envious,
drowned in blood the life of his brother, Abel,
opening a flow of evil
in the channel of the human race;
but his hands, Christ's hands,
transformed that fratricidal path
into a way of eternal brotherhood.

"I would like to have those hands:
hands that pray in the cool dawn
when dew is trembling upon the grass
or the wind sighs in the desert;
hands that pray for the peace of the world,
hands that pray for human grief,
for you and for me;
hands that pray in the face of the radiant sun
before God's glory
in the mountain
seeking the immortal brilliance of the spirit;
hands that pray in the dark night,
in bitter anguish
in the Garden of Olives,
when the stars receive
the message of the triumphant spirit
in face of the inevitable
'not my will but thine, be done.'

"I would like to have those hands:
hands that, the Master on his knees,
lovingly washed the dust of the road
from the disciples' tired feet.
During the long days they had walked wearily
from Galilee of the Gentiles
to the royal Jerusalem.
From there,
weeks afterwards,
they would walk even farther:

to the ends of the earth.
Those hands admonish us,
with urgent example,
to be candid,
to be noble
and to possess true humility
and true integrity.
Although, knowing that he is great,
he uses his greatness with courtly grace
in giving, in serving, in loving.

"I would like to have those hands:
those hands motionless, quiet
before Pilate, the governor of cowardly arrogance,
and Caiaphas, the priest of dramatic cynicism;
hands that refuse to covenant with the mighty
who have his life in their power;
serene and motionless hands,
that say nothing
but proclaim everything
because in their austere silence
the eloquent and sovereign truth is speaking.

"I would like to have those hands:
hands that were immobilized,
nailed on the cross,
hands wounded and bathed in blood,
innocent, generous and pure blood,
that, issuing forth from his wounded body
becomes redemptive in the veins of all humanity
so that they may be purified and cured;
hands that drip red tears
on the human disgrace,
hands that soothe sweetly
the wounds of those who wounded him.

"I would like to have those hands:
hands that rolled the sealed stone of his sepulcher
on the smiling morning of his resurrection

43

when the dewy lilies quivered
as the wings of angels
came from the ethereal regions
to announce to all
that the will of the Son of man
had been stronger and more powerful
than the might of the spirit of evil
and the destructive sickle
of the somber and cruel ruler
of the regions of darkness and death.

"I would like to have those hands:
invisible hands of Jesus,
which, since they arose from the tomb
have followed all the paths of the earth
looking for pearls in the mire
and petals of roses in the wilderness:
resplendent pearls and petals
with which to crown God's head
at the singing of the celestial choir
celebrating the eternal triumph of love
under the brilliant starry arches of the heavens."

This was my secret prayer
in the chapel
while, in front of my eyes
at the altar,
the red roses smiled,
and I sensed through them
the generous, kind hands of Jesus:
roses from the garden of God.
While I was asking this,
silently,
in the soft notes of the organ
I perceived Christ's voice:
    "Why do you want my hands
    if you have yours?
    Do you not know that your hands,

yes, even your feeble hands,
are my hands in the world?
If you do not give them to me
I have no others.
Did I not say to you on that last night
in Jerusalem,
that greater things than I
you would do?
Then my hands did their work
for you.
Now your hands will do their work
for me.
Do not ask me for my hands;
I am the one who asks for your hands.''

In the inner chapel of my being
my lips murmured a silent amen,
and when my petition ceased,
I looked at my poor hands.
It seemed to me that they had,
though just a little,
some resemblance to Jesus' hands;
and as I crossed the threshold of the sanctuary
I had the joyous impression
that they,
like those of the Master,
were opening graciously
to spread in other's paths
the petals of roses
which moments before,
had smiled at me from the altar.

School of Theology
Buenos Aires
April, 1945

45

I Had Never Liked the Pepper Tree

I had never liked
the pepper tree;
it seemed to me too ordinary
and lacking in charm
till I went up to the desert land of Atacama*
where no other tree thrives.
And there I saw that tree
—it alone—
adorning streets, plazas, and patios;
and in its humble garb,
I saw it offering its greenness and shade
to the sandy soil.

Then, and there, I loved and blessed
the pepper tree,
and I prayed to be like it:
to be of consolation and hope
where there is none
to inspire fortitude and peace.

Chuquicamata, Chile.
July 7, 1947

Atacama is a desert in Northern Chile.

Together

I felt great pity to see you both like that
—the two of you so alone—
at the edge of the road
lost in the immensity of the Atacama desert,
O pepper trees!

Alone,
in that vastness
and with those sad branches
so heavily covered with dust,
you were begging the people passing
for mercy and some cool water from a singing fountain.

I felt pity for you;
but immediately I consoled myself
thinking
that it would be a crueler fate
if there were just one tree
instead of two,
in that melancholy, sandy land
at the edge of the roadway.

Because between the two,
the pains of one serve as balm to the other.
Because sorrows are not so deep and piercing
when we feel them and carry them together!

Chuquicamata, Chile
July 7, 1947

Stay with Us

"Sir, stay with us!"
the disciples of the Emmaus road begged
the resurrected Master,
who had walked with them
without disclosing himself.
The evening shadows were falling on the village
when he, to please them, went into their home
to rest and dine with them.
When he gave thanks
and broke bread
they recognized him.
Then he slipped away.
He had to meet other pilgrims,
travelers of this life
and of the wide world
and of other ages,
who would also need to share
his friendship and revelation.

Christ is still walking Emmaus roads,
where he always meets those who ask him,
as in those ancient days,
"Sir, stay with us!"
Will he stay with you, friend,
if you want to detain him?
Who knows?
Let us go with him to some of those encounters
in modern times
perhaps in your own city.

A great multitude filled the cathedral.
The candles were burning on the altar,
the choir was singing elaborating alleluias
while the priest officiated before the altar.

Suddenly,
without their knowing from where,
a man, plainly dressed,
with calloused hands
came toward the high altar.
Under the curious and disapproving gaze
of the multitude
he approached the priest,
who interrupted his ceremony
to ask the intruder,
"Who are you and what to you want at the Lord's altar?"
"I am Jesus of Nazareth,
and I am looking for people willing to follow me."
He showed him the nail wounds in his hands.
"O Lord!" said the priest, "Stay with us!
All of this great crowd will adore and exalt you."
"I cannot remain.
The Son of man did not come to be served
but to serve
and to give his life as a ransom for many.
There on the far off mountain, there are suffering souls
who cry out in wretched huts;
there where few dare to go, I go
to be health and hope for their lives.
I want to know if you are willing to go with me!"

The young doctor, filled with dreams,
a recent graduate of the university,
was practicing his profession in a big, modern hospital
hidden in the midst of luxuriant trees.
He was hoping to be promoted
to department head
and to reach great renown as a master of surgery
or as a genius in the science of giving prescriptions.
At the end of a pleasant evening,
after hard labor,
he was relaxing under the foliage.
A humble man, dressed in working clothes,

49

approached him,
and abruptly asked:
"Are you a physician?"
"Yes, can I help you?"
Showing him the nail wounds in his hands, the newcomer
    said,
"Are you able to cure these deep wounds?"
Kneeling before Jesus, the doctor cried out;
"Lord, stay with me!
Your presence alone will provide us with miraculous
    power."
"No, I cannot remain," said the Master, "you come with
    me!
In far away regions of your beloved land,
in forests, mountains, and dark valleys,
there are innumerable, suffering bodies and souls
who demand your kind and skillful hands
and your whole life, as if it were mine.
I wish to know if you are willing to go there with me!"

On a pleasant spring morning
the young heart of the teacher was in tune
with the joyful singing of the birds.
Her dream, as an ambitious girl
bent over her books,
and her glimpes of a future full of honors
had been fulfilled.
Now she faced those restless children
of that prestigious neighborhood
in a beautiful school.
She was looking at her pupils
almost with a maternal air;
they gave her the impression
that they were like restless birds
thoughtlessly pecking at seeds of wisdom.
It was a difficult task
to convince them that letters and numbers were more
    useful

than running after butterflies
or paddling in the clear waters of a brook!
Suddenly, to the great surprise of the pupils,
the lesson was interrupted by a stranger.
"Good morning, my lady, and forgive me if I am
    intruding."
"Come in, sir. What do you desire?"
"I am visiting the city, and, by chance, this school."
"Are you a state school inspector?
You will see how alive and intelligent these children are.
Stand up! Greet our visitor!
But, can you tell us your name, sir,
so that we may know what to call you?"
With a gentle sign, he asked the children to sit down
and with a soft voice, he answered:
"I am not really a school inspector;
nevertheless, I was a teacher, and still am.
If I wanted to, I could give you lessons of geography
and history,
because I know very well where people wander
and their stubborn and foolish adventures.
But I cannot, I am engaged in many other duties,
and my name you do know.
I am Jesus of Nazareth!"
"Jesus of Nazareth. Our Lord!" the teacher shouted.
"My desk is yours. Tell us your beautiful stories!
You are welcome! Stay with us!
We shall keep your lessons in our hearts."
But Jesus, approaching the doorway, said,
"I cannot stay in this pleasant place;
in the poor quarters of this same city
in lost villages at the foot of far away mountains,
in scattered settlements and in forests,
I have seen thousands of children
dirty and ragged, without shoes,
without schools, without teachers, without a future.
I am going to them to tell them my stories.

51

I want to know if you desire to go there with me
and transform those ragged beings into men and women.''

The young, ambitious architect was eagerly engaged
in drawing plans for an enormous skyscraper
which would be located on the main avenue
where the financial market pulsated with life
and exerted its influence.
The night was far gone and the drawings unfinished,
and the architect, unaware of the passing hours,
was working tirelessly on.
That building would bring him remuneration and honor!
It was already midnight, according to the tower of the
    cathedral,
when he heard someone knocking at the door.
Who would interrupt him at such an unusual hour of the
    night?
When he opened the door he faced a humble workman
who had with him a carpenter's square and a hammer.
Bruskly the architect confronted him:
''Are you coming to look for work at this hour?
I am not available, I am involved in profound study.''
He was about to shut the door in the face of the intruder.
''Don't dismiss in this way the carpenter of Nazareth!
I did not study in famous schools,
but I, too, am an expert in construction.''
''Jesus of Nazareth, forgive me!
Teacher of universal engineering, stay with me!
Like an unexpected blessing you have arrived here
to help me solve the difficult problem
of raising with mastery an immense building of cement
    and granite,
in the very center of our great city.''
But the Galilean carpenter answered:
''I am not seeking work; I have abundant work.
What is troubling me is a very different matter.
In the poor quarters of this great city
I have seen many men, women, and children;

52

there are no avenues, gardens, or plazas,
those people live crowded in shanties, without air or light.
It is necessary to build many small dwellings,
which will have air and light, and yards for the children,
and clean kitchens where mothers can cook with joy
the proper food for their children,
and the husbands can relax their bodies and spirits
when they return from their daily work.
Skyscrapers, my young friend, we have enough already.
We urgently need to build villages and cities
in the countryside, suitable houses for the millions
who do not possess them.
God did not create this world of ours
for some to get rich building skyscrapers
and others to suffer in vile poverty.
I came to see if you are willing to help me!''

And, while we were going with the Master on this
    pilgrimage
seeing such extraordinary visions,
certainly, we learned the urgent request
we should send to heaven.
We will no longer say, ''Master, stay with us!''
Your prayer and mine will be:
''Wherever you want me to go
in this big world,
Lord,
for you, I will go.
Where my life will be most needed
to carry your name and your love,
Lord,
for you, I will go.''
Then, it will not be necessary to ask for his presence,
because, truly, the Master will stand at our side.

Huancayo, Perú
July 29, 1947

53

Enchanted Night

Summer night,
　magnificent night,
　　moonlit night.
Serenity penetrates the twilight,
at midnight the city rests.
The moon bathes everything in silent light.
I put out the lamp,
　and open the window
　　and I lie down exhausted.
I cannot sleep,
　O beautiful night!
　　Enchanted night!
I gaze at the night,
which enters my chamber on tiptoe
shining night,
　fragrant night,
　　enchanted night!
I keep watch in the night
　through the window
　　and I hear the murmur of the wind
　　　in the trees,
soft wind,
　wind that gently goes by,
　　wind that softly hums.
It hums among the leaves,
　and among the flowers,
　　and in my soul:
Song of the wind coming from afar
　where it seeks distant shores.
Nostalgic sigh
　which carries away my longings.
Word of God whispering
in the night,

Word of God in my chamber, speaking to my soul,
which wants to repose
and cannot:
because the night is soft,
  exquisite
    and quiet.
Enchanted night!

How could my soul rest on such a night?
In the stillness
a divine voice speaks to me.

With a casual look
  I contemplate the sky
    and discover a shining star.
Suspended in infinite space
it also spies me:
pure light,
  silent light,
    divine light.
God's light penetrating through the window
into my chamber:
light scattering stanzas of eternity,
inexpressible poetry of the vastness
spread by the hand of God!
Symphony of the night.
Poetry of God's spirit!
Enchanted night!
A night for meeting God;
to adore him,
  and in silence
    to hear his voice,
and to fill the soul with enchantment and gentleness

Light of stars in my chamber,
poetry of God in my soul!
I breathe the air through the window:
fresh air,

    melodious air,
      scented air.
The white flowers of the night,
    that slept during the day
      enraptured by the sunshine,
are perfuming the air.
Perfume, exhaling serenity,
    caressing serenity,
      caress of subtle, ethereal sensitivity
caress of God in the soul,
    caress of perfume,
      perfume of caress;
fragrance of God in the quietness,
in my chamber.
Enchanted night!

Flowers climbing the wall of the garden,
flowers ascending through the windows of my soul!

The wind ceases to sing
    among the leaves
      and around the flowers.
Now, through the window
    in serene peace
      I hear the murmur of the fountain.
Water from the mountain.
    cuts through rocks
      and weeds,
in the perfumed night.
Everything sleeps,
    the water is vigilant and running.
Rest it does not know.
It mumbles
    day and night,
      the yearning of its soul:
like God, its Father and mine,
who never sleeps,
and who, now,

in the murmur of the water, reveals his love
in my chamber.
Enchanted night!

Song of the mountain water among the rocks.
Song of God among the dreams of my soul!

The wind,
   the star,
      the perfume,
         the water,
are singing a melodious ballad
in the night,
a prayer of serenity in my heart,
invoking sleep
   invoking calmness.

I resist going to sleep,
the night is so bewitching!
But in my upper room
my Father God
invites me
to rest.
I close my eyes and hear his voice:
   "Son, sleep and rest,
   soon dawn will be here;
   when the sun arises
   on the mountain,
   your fellowmen
   will demand beauty from your soul
   and, from your hand, labor.''

I can no longer resist,
I open my eyes
and comtemplate again the perfumed night.
As I close my eyes,
over my brow comes a mysterious flutter.
Someone is kissing my soul:
kiss of peace of divine love,

in the quiet and enchanting night,
before my silent wandering
through mystical regions of dreams.

Enchanted night!
  God has been in my chamber!

> *At the foot of the mountains of Santa Maria,*
> *Río Grande, Brazil*
> *March 9, 1947, 2:30 A.M.*

If You Have a Word of Encouragement

If you have a word of encouragement to speak,
speak it.
Speak it without delay,
gently
with love
and as if you were not speaking it;
speak it as if you were caressing the soul
which is waiting for a voice of encouragement.
Say it as God would say it
to the solitary being,
who at the fall of night
is listening to the murmur of the water which flows
under the bridge
toward the sea.

If you have a word of inspiration to say
speak it
say it softly.
Say it with discretion
and without pretension.
Say it with a smile on your lips

and another in your soul,
like the song of a bird at dawn,
fresh, joyful, compassionate, caressing,
like a song vibrating in the smiling drop of dew.

If you have a consoling word to speak,
speak it.
Speak it without delay
gently,
lovingly,
as if your voice were walking on tiptoe
and full of love,
without humiliating the aching and sensitive soul.
Say it with such a soft voice
that it may quell the sharpness of anguish
and may refresh
like drops of dew woven in serenity
over the perfumed roses of the morning.

If you have a forgiving word to say,
say it.
Say it without rancorous remembrances
and recriminations,
forgetting the past,
as if through your word would flow
all the immeasurable harmony
of a soul that conveys compassion.
Say it with such an assuring voice
that the one who wounded you
will know undoubtedly that, in your voice,
the voice of a friend is speaking.

If you have a just and truthful word to say,
say it.
Say it openly,
forcefully
with all your soul,
without considering the cost

without shunning sacrifice.
Say it with the transparency of things
which cannot be hidden,
But say it, in a tone
which never would be used
from enemy to enemy,
like a savage, deadly spear
that wounds, wrecks, and destroys.
Say it as if it were soothing medicine
transfused with care, from your heart
to the soul of your brother
with the fervent desire to rescue him from error
and to make him a devotee of the Eternal Truth.

If you have a word of love to say,
say it.
Say it as if it were your best offering to God,
your highest creation of life,
the most sublime singing of your heart,
the highest aspiration of your being.
Say it with your soul on your lips,
as if you desired to perpetuate all your yearnings in it,
and with rhapsody, infuse it
into the grief of those who hear
all your deep and noble dreams.
Say it with a feeling so sincere
that those who hear it
may hear in your voice, the echo
of that boundless love,
which, unfathomable,
was converted into a sacrificial flower
on the somber cruel arms of a cross.

If you have, therefore, a word to speak,
speak it,
but say it always with dignity
as if, through your lips, God himself were speaking.

January 23, 1947

When Your Life Seems Burdened

When your life seems too burdened
and unbearable
and your inner being fraught with anxieties,
venture through the open fields
and fix your gaze on the distant horizons.
Throw your bitter soul into the singing
and restless waters
of a clear, swift brook;
open your heavy heart to the free winds,
and let the mud of the fields stick to your shoes.
Afterwards, bow your troubled spirit
under a whispering tree
and in intimate and solitary confession
disburden before God,
your merciful Father,
your secret grief
and your deep pain.
Then go back to your daily tasks;
and, resounding in your soul,
you will find the new song of hope and faith
which will diffuse itself in a rain of white petals
through the distressing wilderness of your life.

Illinois, U.S.A.
March 29–30, 1951

And the Word Became Flesh

John 1:14

Flesh of our flesh you made yourself,
O Christ,
Word of God,
light of light which illuminated the darkness
of centuries that never were
and the obscurity of our uncreated souls.

Make yourself the throbbing Word,
O Christ,
in our flesh:
the living word, which clamors
in our breast,
from the depth of your creative passion
to the height of your enduring compassion.

Make yourself the singing Word in our soul,
O Christ,
the word which displays your beauty
in verses of translucent white light,
light from the heart of God.

Make yourself the buoyant Word in our life,
O Christ,
the word-sea of boundless shores
which may hurl with rushing frenzy
against the reefs of time
the foam of dreams woven with eternal threads.

O Word of God,
make yourself word in our mortal flesh;
flesh of our sepulcher,
make yourself a temple of the Word of God.

La Paz, Bolivia
1951

Cactus Flower

Among the scorched and dusty stones,
you were born,
cactus flower!
The cool, soft dew,
silent tears of the night
drenched with the light of stars,
wasted away into the dryness of the soil
and lost itself,
to give you birth.

Now you smile under the sun,
yellow flower,
offspring of sacrifice
and of all-enduring charity.
O smile, smiling in light,
giving yourself,
you beseech us with a plea of love
to bring forth, out of the stony land of our life,
harmony and color
and beauty.

In your singing loveliness,
cactus flower,
dressed in morning light,
you proclaim the triumph of sorrow become victory.
Bring forth, O life of mine,
from the rocks, flowers,
and smiles from the sandy land!

Cochabama, Bolivia
November 18, 1953

Listening to the Sea

Does the sea speak?
What language does it use
when it preaches in the midst of the beauty
of infinity?
Does the water speak,
or the abyss,
or the wind,
or God,
or all of them,
and do we, too?
Is this the yearning voice
of the universe?
Who can speak?

Speak out, O prophet!
No, the prophet cannot speak:
'Tis a voice beyond prophecy.
Speak out, O dreamer!
Are your dreams
like the dreams of the sea,
which crash in the sand
in a laughter of foam?
How can you speak of the dreams of the sea
if you cannot reveal to our ears
the deep visions
of your yearning soul?
O soul of the sea,
soul of our soul!
O universal language of what was
and is
and shall forever be!

Murmuring, murmuring, murmuring.
What do you say?
O mystery of my mystery,

O abyss of my soul,
O song of my longings,
O clamor of my dreams!

Through the jumbled words of the sea
a boat with white sails
is escaping.
O pilgrim boat, carried by the wind,
are you going away,
far away,
in search of new worlds?
Do you not know
that at the bottom,
in the very depth
in everything sublime
and noble,
there is only one key word?
'Tis the magic word
which unlocks
the way to and from mystery.
'Tis love.
If you can grasp the meaning
of love,
you will understand the voice of the sea.
Because love is the voice of God,
and God speaks in everything,
everywhere.

Come back, yes, come back
O boat of the white sails,
take me in.
Take me away!
Let us sail the seven seas
singing
with the wind
and the waves
the eternal song
of the boundless love of God

in Christ,
until every human tongue
will sing in tune,
and hate shall be no more,
and peace and joy will sit
at the doorstep
of every home
of our humanity.

Dakar, Senegal, Africa
November 18, 1954

Kindness

"Love is kind."
1 Corinthians 13:4

"Do not let your left hand know
what your right hand is doing,"
exhorts the voice from the mountain.
Love will fall on the wounded soul
or on the sick body,
like the fresh dew of the rising morning,
without voices,
or words,
silently,
softly.

It will come and go
like the soft breeze
which comes singing mysteries.
And takes away
sobbing
from your soul

and from mine
without ever revealing to indiscrete ears
the reason for our anguish.

It will shine in our faces
like the silent light
of stars
in the quiet night:
light which glows
without wounding the eyes:
light which sings
without wounding the nerves:
light which caresses,
whispering hope within the soul.

It touches our tired feet
like the smooth wave
of the singing river
which comes and goes,
and loses itself in the distance,
spreading freshness
and harmony
without waiting
for thanks.

It is the hand which writes our condemnation
in the sand,
so that the wind
will erase it
and time will forget it.
It is harmony which comes
from fingers that play invisibly
lullabies of our destiny,
on the harp strings of time,
which extends itself from eternity to eternity.
Love of God made into grace:
love which dresses the lilies of the field
and feeds the little birds of heaven;

which speaks in the very core of our being
with a soft voice,
with the voice of Christ:
"Neither do I condemn you;
go,
and sin no more."

Buenos Aires, Argentina, 1959

Look at the Birds of the Air

"As for knowledge, it will pass away."
1 Corinthians 13:8

Blessed Christ, who in thy simplicity
didst order us to look at the lilies of the fields
and at the little birds of heaven:
thou knowest that there is no science
except God's;
the science which weaves in the silence of beauty
and in the beauty of silence
the white lilies
and the swift wings of the little birds.

What didst thou want us to learn,
O Christ,
except that we should trust more in God
than in ourselves?
And more in God's protective love
than in our vain pride?
Flowers and birds,
colors and wings,
perfumes and songs,
what are they next to atomic missiles

and the skyscrapers of steel and cement?
The voice of our century clamors:
look to the marvels of our modern world,
the world created by us,
the world of laboratories
and of burning furnaces!
Poor, crazy Jesus,
romantic and dreaming soul
who invites us to look at
the grass which today is
and tomorrow has withered,
and the wing which today flies,
and tomorrow will rest in the dump pile!

But from heaven, God sees our arrogance
and, through Christ's lips,
asks us,
"Why are you afraid?"
Yes, we are afraid of our knowledge
because in its bosom
resounds the sonorous and malicious
laughter of Satan.
He has taken us prisoners in our pride,
made us his slaves
so as to bury us
with rage and hate
under the cement and steel
of our apostate civilization.
We are wise and powerful
with the secrets which we have stolen
from the bosom of mother nature.
But we are afraid, yea, very afraid,
and we watch one another
with lynx' eyes
and the treachery of hyenas.
What of the Sermon on the Mount?
'Tis fantasy!

However, we should hear the words of warning:
"Heaven and earth shall pass away
but my word shall not."

Yes, in the blossom of the flowers
and in the song of the birds
there is eternal wisdom,
deeper than Solomon's mind,
higher than the distance of the stars.
What is our truth
but the shadow of things which we see?
When God's day will come,
everything which is ours
will be darkness
and only God's word
will be truth
because it rises from the depth of love.
Without love there is no truth.
There can be only arrogance
and abuse
and fear.
"Look at the birds of the air!"

Buenos Aires, Argentina, 1959

Make Love Your Aim

"Make love your aim."
1 Corinthians 14:1

Follow,
pursue,
deepen,
disrupt,
your love.
Possess love,
make it the passion of your soul,
light of your eyes,
action of your hand
vision of your vigils,
yearning of your life.

May it bubble up in your bosom
as the water of the sea
which breaks against the reefs
or sings on the shore,
or murmurs before the immensity
of the horizon!

May it sing on your lips
like a whisper between leaves
on a springtime morning
or a fall evening:
a mixture of longing and hope,
between what was
and what will be;
a song of dormant dreams
transformed into the reality of eternity
and the radiance of glory!

Forge with it
and with patient art
the task of your hand.

O gracious task
which incites the receiver
with the unrest of your eagerness
converted into blessing
and challenge!

Take it with you
in the street
in the office;
or wherever you go
as comforting incense
at the bed of pain
or in the anguished home
or in the solitary corner
where the abandoned soul
exhausts itself in the desperation
of defeat
and solitude.
And, even when you are crucified,
like your Master,
let the tears of your blood be
the dew of pardon,
and the last words of your lips,
a prayer of mercy
for the redemption of those who,
despising you,
are destroying you.
They will not kill you, though.
Out of the sepulcher into which
they will put you,
you will be raised
because love is the essence
of the divine,
which carries in its bosom
the immortal spark of the eternal becoming.

Buenos Aires, Argentina, 1959

Flowers of Sacrifice

The aging woman with a wrinkled face,
crossing the train tracks
that warm sunny morning,
had an unexpressive and vague look;
but on her frail and bent shoulders
she carried a basket overflowing with flowers;
and, as she went,
she scattered smiles made of silky petals
and a subtle fragrance of mixed sweet scents.

The basket which she carried
was her grief
and her glory;
her eyes were full of sorrow and pain
her weary steps were heavy,
but upon her bent shoulders bloomed abundant grace!

There are men
and women in this world of ours
who pour comforting grace
into the bosom of other lives,
but must carry shadows in their own eyes,
agony in their own hearts,
and wrinkles in their faces.

Blessed are those who, without complaint,
carry on their shoulders,
bent by grief and pain,
a basket overflowing with petals and sweet perfumes.

Buenos Aires, Argentina
January, 1960

Insuperable Love

Till the end you loved us, O Christ.
What does it mean to love *till the end?*
Till death or beyond the sepulcher?
You do not have beginning or end,
love of our love and life of our life!
You loved us beyond our understanding,
reaching to the bottom of our souls
—our deep and unfathomable abyss!—
and, from there, with the patience of a fisher for pearls,
you sought our pain and deathly venom
and all that converts it into horror and shame
and you opened up a fountain of purifying waters.

O fresh, singing, eternal waters
in which are mingled the tears of your compassion
and the soft murmuring of your boundless grace!
Your love, Christ of love,
is the humility that cleanses the dust
from our straying feet
which wander through the varied paths of the world;
it is grief that purifies our souls in your blood
shed on the rugged arms of a cross;
it is sympathy that follows us where no one will rescue us
except your hand wounded by our own iniquity
and by your infinite compassion.
Love of our love, love that loves us till the end,
redeem us from our egoism,
from our hatred
from our passions!
Let us die on your cross!
Let us live in your life!
Let us be immortalized in the splendor of your glory!

La Paz, Bolivia
December 9, 1952

Sublimity

"Hold fast to what is good."
Romans 12:9

When you came, O Christ,
creating in us abhorrence
of the despicable
and transient,
you did not want to separate us from the world
and from people.
You also interceded for us
when with your first disciples you asked,
"I do not pray, Father,
that you should take them out of the world,
but that you should keep them
from the evil one."
You prayed that we might detest evil
while remaining in the world:
be lights,
stars
illuminating the path of others
towards the sublime life of God.
You not only created in us
a hatred for evil,
O Christ,
you invited us to hold fast to the good;
you do not want to see in us
only denial,
the No!
You aspire to find in our life
also affirmation,
the Yes!
creative exuberance.
sublimity,
exaltation.

Where shall we find the power
to transfer our abhorrence
to the attraction of the noble life
and to the affirmation of our ego?
How can we flee from ''the body of death''?
You, yourself, O Christ,
suggest it to us:
''I am the true vine,
you are the branches,
apart from me you can do nothing.''
Saint Paul confirmed it
when he affirmed in the Roman prison,
''I can do all things
in Christ who strengthens me.''

No, no one has sufficient power
to hold fast to the good
except by holding fast to you,
O Christ:
only when one is fused and made one with you
in flesh and spirit,
so that what one feels
is no more his own will,
but your spirit,
yes, your own life:
only then will he have the strength
to be
what he should be.

O Life of our life
O Love of our love
O Glory of our glory!

Abhorrence and affirmation should become
only one thing,
like two sides
of a coin.
They cannot be separated.
Our No! has to be succeeded with our Yes!

so that "seven other bad spirits"
may not take the place
of the one which was expelled,
and the sanctuary of our heart,
—clean and finely adorned
with new light—
may not be occupied again
by the one which is always waiting
for a chance to envelop us
and make us fall.
Let us hold fast to what is good,
abhorring evil,
so that the Holy Spirit may enter us
and nourish the tree of life
bringing forth good fruits
which feed the blood of the soul:
love,
  joy,
    light,
      compassion,
        gentleness,
goodness,
  faith,
    meekness,
      sobriety.
O Christ, take us by our hand,
so that abhorrence may not exhaust us
and enthusiasm may not blind us!
At the urging of your firm steps,
help us to forge ahead,
to climb the rough slope,
go to the top,
and to glimpse in the shining sky
the eternal path that faith reveals
and love constructs.

Buenos Aires, Argentina, 1967

An Encounter

You, O God,
yesterday,
in the plane which was carrying me
across the United States,
seated me by the side of a young officer
of the North American army.

I looked at him with anguish,
thinking of Vietnam.

After a long silence,
while I was examining him
with inquiring curiosity,
and considering the handsomeness of his uniform
and the shining insignia,
I dared timidly to speak
to him.

"Where are you coming from,
young man?"
"From Germany," he replied.
"Are you going to return there?"
"No" he answered.
"I shall go to Vietnam."
My anguish soaked deeper
in my soul
and in my mind I saw that young man
blown into pieces
under a bomb.

So virile he was,
so neat
so sure of himself.
Nevertheless destined to kill
and to die!
I gently pressed his arm

as a father to a son,
and I spoke again,
"God keep you safe!"
Then I fell into silence.
I could not say more.
Within me my soul
was weeping.

So impotent we are
to end this terrible war!

After a while I told him that
some of us
had tried to stop this war
appealing to the political powers,
but without success.

He answered me:
"It will not last long!"

"May God hear you!"
I said within myself.

When he got up
to leave the plane
he smiled
and said to me,
"Good luck, sir!"

How sadly resounded in my heart
that gentle wish of his!

My anguish went even deeper
into my soul.
O anguish sharp
of my helplessness.
It was the anguish
of a Christian
who shares with many others
the guilt
for this incomprehensible war

in Vietnam.
I was conscious,
while I saw him go
that I was sharing
with the rest of my generation
its foolishness,
its impotence,
its crimes,
and that I was surely thrusting
a sword
in the back of
that young man
whom we were sending out
to kill
and to die.
I remembered his parting words:
"Good luck, sir!"
And I pondered:
Did I deserve it?
Did we deserve it?

O Lord, have mercy on us,
and forgive us,
to whom you entrusted
a Gospel of life
yes, to us,
who are announcing
to the rest of the world
with terrible deeds
a message of death
and destruction!

Galveston, Texas, U.S.A.
March 29, 1968

Martin Luther King

You, a new Christian martyr,
   Martin Luther King,
have fallen under the blind violence
of hate,
   prejudice
     and injustice.

But it was not only you
who has fallen;
in another way
the one who foolishly dared
to kill you
has fallen too
into the trap of our millennial prejudice
and hate.

You have left our history,
leaving behind you a path
which will not be closed.
It is marked by your blood
and the blood,
   and tears,
     and hopes
of a great legion
of modern heroes of the faith.
With you, Martin Luther King,
Another died.
He died again
as he has died millions of times
together with those who have loved
him
and his kingdom.

He was the first one to preach love
in the face of violence,

and violence killed him also
but not his love!
He left the marks of his life
upon a cross:
it is the cross that you took up
also.
Though your calvary, Martin Luther King,
was like an unexpected shot,
it sounds in our ears
the blasphemy
of our disturbed and confused age.
We are not mature as yet:
the claws of the brute are hidden
within our gloves,
and our skyscrapers are built upon
the caves of our savage heredity.

The voice of Christ is covered up
by the vibrations of the atomic missiles
and the exploitation of the market place
where the tears and blood of humanity
are still bought and sold.

You have not died
in vain,
Martin Luther King.
But have you indeed died?
Did not the Master say
that those who give up their lives
for his cause
will live forever?

We salute you,
this day of your coronation,
Martin Luther King!
We see you marching ahead
of us.
There is brilliance in your face,

and like Stephen of old
your eyes are fixed toward heaven
where there is prepared a reception
for you.
Standing,
with luminous eyes,
the Son of man is ready to greet you
and we hear his voice
saying;
"Well done, my faithful servant,
enter into the glory of my Kingdom!"

You are entering the domain
of his eternity,
but we are still here.
We still have to end our march.
Oh, that we may not hide
in the wayside bushes
while the struggle goes on.

May we march,
guided by the footprints you left
behind you,
may we hear the voice
of the Commander,
    "Be not afraid,
    I have conquered the world,
    and I will be with you
    till the end of the age!"

What a terrible,
but a glorious feat it is
to march in the company of such a Commander!

Galveston, Texas, U.S.A.
April 4, 1968
Day of his assassination in Memphis, Tennessee

Anguish

"I thirst."
John 19:28

Your disparing cry,
"I thirst"
still vibrates on the sound waves
of the world
and of history.
O hurt-rendering thirst!
They gave you
vinegar,
to calm your anguish.
Vinegar,
   vinegar,
     vinegar!
We always give you,
vinegar to drink,
in return for the sweet wine
of your immeasurable tenderness!

What was your thirst?
Certainly your body was burning with fever
and you felt your lips parting
with a tormenting dryness,
but, really your thirst was of another kind
thirst of your soul,
thirst and hunger for justice
like that of all the prophets
who came before you.
It was the thirst which accompanied you
on the roads of Palestine,
in the temple
   and synagogue,
on mountains
   and plains,

among Pharisees and doctors of the Law,
in the Sanhedrin
   and in Pilate's palace:
soul-breaking thirst,
   unquenchable
      tormenting thirst.
No one could quench that thirst,
because nobody offered you
the kind of drink
capable of satiating it,
but you quenched the thirst
of so many souls
along your path.

"Give me a drink,"
you asked a Samaritan woman
one day,
who went to draw water
out of Jacob's well
in Samaria,
but you did not drink
of that water.
Before you was a woman
thirsty for pure love
but lost in profane affection.
and you forgot your physical thirst
and gave her of the water
"which wells up to eternal life."
You freed her of her insatiable
worldly thirst
and gave wings to her spirit,
and liberated her from an obsessive tyranny
and made her into a spring
of pure water
for her fellow-citizens,
who in turn came to drink
of the inexhaustible well of your love.

You also offered
freely
of your water
to the citizens of Jerusalem
and with a strong voice
you challenged them to drink:
"If anyone thirsts,
come to me
and drink.
If anyone believes in me,
out of his heart
shall flow rivers of living water."
But to you,
on that cross,
to you who offered
rivers of living water,
those same citizens of Jerusalem
gave you vinegar to drink
with all the bitter taste
of all the rottenness of the world.
And you died with your thirst,
with that tremendous thirst of your soul
which no one understood
and which no one satisfied.
That vinegar sealed
your death,
death which sealed your thirst for love
and justice.
You are still wandering
throughout the world
knocking at the doors of our homes,
wanting to come in
to eat with us
and to drink of the cup
of peace.
But we offer you the many
drinks

which we crave
and which you refuse to accept.
We invite you to banquets
which your soul abhors,
and compliment you
with frenetic and impudent toasts.
But you, pilgrim of all roads,
patiently persist
in offering us your cup,
which, when we drink,
converts us into the only thing
which quenches
your thirst.
O thirst of God
    for our love!

Miami, Florida, U.S.A.
1972

While Night Comes . . .

"My soul yearns for thee in the night,
my spirit within me earnestly seeks thee.
For when thy judgments are in the earth,
the inhabitants of the world learn righteousness."
Isaiah 26:9

I open the newspapers to encounter
the world, near and far;
and what was there yesterday,
   I find again today:
distrust,
   strife,
      destruction,
         death.
Hate is running wild
in the countryside,
   mountains
      and cities;
it is violence without mercy:
the four horsemen of the Apocalypse
multiplying themselves,
and on the horses
no longer men are riding
but hyenas and tigers
mangling
   and tearing open human bodies
for the vultures
   and carrions.
This is the exalted century
of brilliant lights
of omnipotent science,
of computers,
of television,

of interplanetary flights
and of sky explorers
traveling months
   and even years
through unlimited space
to find out what there is on the other planets
and if there are beings like us.
   May God help those beings
   to behave better than we!

Oh that we could yet attract
God's angels,
those angels who bring peace
and goodwill,
as that distant night
when they proclaimed Jesus' coming!
But the air is too defiled
and they cannot breathe
with so many gases
and chemicals
and burning of forests;
the sight in some regions
of our earth
is desolate
and shocking,
with so many millions of craters opened
by bombs
and splashed with human blood
and smoking with hate.

Those horrified servants of God
have covered their eyes
with their wings
because they have exhausted
their tears;
and their lips have become silent
with the distressing silence of millions
of premature corpses.

It is becoming more and more dangerous
and compromising
to have any dealings with humanity
who has not as yet removed
the crosses
from the Golgothas,
the gallows
from the crossroads.

How we have disregarded
Christ's voice
that invites us to learn
from him
and to be like him,
gentle,
    loving
        and long-suffering!

The shadows of the evening
are descending,
the clouds,
rose tinged,
pass over the roofs,
and the tops of the pine trees
close to my windows
are at rest.
I fold the newspapers
with disgust in my soul
and I try to meditate.
To ponder, on what,
my God?

In my ears are still resounding
the echoes of the firearms
coming from a nearby military camp,
where young men are taught to become
excellent instruments of death
and destruction.
Will they,

yes, my sons and grandchildren,
learn to kill, one of these days?
O my God!
This thought paralyzes me;
will these angels of my flesh
likewise become demons
tomorrow?

There is a tempest
within me;
and I cannot,
no, I cannot conceive,
that these my grandchildren,
so simple and innocent,
will someday handle firearms
to kill
and to die.

"Let them come to me,"
says the Master,
but we give them
other tutors
and schooling.
We are ashamed
of his word
and cross.
And we write SCIENCE
instead of GOD!

We shall be crammed full with things
to the point of disgust,
and after that, what?
There will be a void,
a bitter taste,
a sour stomach,
and the way leading to the abyss
of nothingness.

Silence!
I need silence;
but the birds are coming back
from their daily pilgrimages
and settling down in the pine trees.
They are talking the sweet language of God,
and in this simple conversation
in the midst of the world's tumult
my soul rests
in silent prayer.
But suddenly a voice emerges
from my silence
"Look at the birds of the air:
they neither sow,
   nor reap,
     nor gather into barns,
and yet your heavenly Father feeds them.
Are you not of more value
than they?"

The birds are quiet,
wrapped in the evening shadows.
Gazing to the high skies,
let us wait, therefore,
hoping that from this darkness
God may send the light of another star,
another star of Bethlehem,
so that the angels may resume
their singing,
and children may come again
to sit on Jesus' lap.

El Palomar, Buenos Aires, Argentina
Wintery Evening, July 24, 1972

Sons of Dust?

Thus the prayer
began
coldly
in remembrance of the friend
who had gone to knock
at the eternal door:
"We confess
to be children
of dust."
Was the dear friend,
gone from our presence,
indeed
  dust?

Am I,
  are you,
    are all of us
dust?

No!
The love of his mother
  and father
that brought him to life
was not DUST!
Was the love
of his teachers
  friends
  and comrades
  just dust?

Human life never is
dust
in God's mind
  and Christ's sacrifice.

The work of our hand,
the thought of our mind,
the brilliant visions of our spirit,
the renewed hope
  of an ascending path,
    never
    are dust.

Dust is
scattered by the wind,
absorbed by the earth,
destroyed by fire,
devoured by the abyss.

Dust is
  form,
  bubble,
  whirlwind,
  sigh,
  complaint,
  echo.

This friend
left behind him
only
the deteriorating image
of his external abode.

But he became
  wind,
  flight,
  distance,
  eternity,
  symphony,
  jubilant chimes
  ringing under the infinite dome
  of God's temple.

His was the triumph
   of pain
against flesh,
and of time
against death.

Never dust,
always spirit,
always eternal love,
the perennial love
   of God.

He is gone, yes,
after the never-ending conquest
of the immeasurable universe!

Montclair, New Jersey, U.S.A.
November 11–12, 1975

Blessed Christ!

"Hosanna! Blessed be he who
comes in the name of the Lord!"
Mark 11:9

Yes, Lord, you are blessed!
Blessed be your coming
   and your name
      and your kingdom!
Blessed be your heart,
   and your hands
      and your feet!
Blessed be all your person!
Alleluia,
   and glory
      and honor!
Heaven
   and earth
      and sea
praise your holy name!
Let us sing harmonious
   joyful,
      ringing
praises,
because your Kingdom
is not that of David
nor of Jerusalem
but of God.
The Eternal Kingdom
embedded in the universal love
of the Father of all humanity,
of Jews and Greeks,
Blacks,
   Yellows,
      Whites.

Hosanna
  glory
    and alleluia
to you,
flesh of our flesh
and hope of our hope
and love of our life;
to you
who did exchange the throne of David
for the heavy burden of our sin,
and who enthroned yourself on the back of the meek colt
of your renunciation
and surrender!

Blessed be you,
O Christ,
forever and ever,
you, who are still riding
on the meek donkey of time
and dismounting at the thresholds of our houses,
to invite us
to participate in the wondrous deeds
of your Spirit!

Buenos Aires, Argentina, 1978

Have Faith in God

Jesus answered them, "Have faith in God."
Mark 11:22

How often, O Lord Jesus,
you invite us to believe
in God!
We forget that God is our strength,
   the support
      and vision
of our life.
You said it in the parable
of the vine and the branches:
we cannot be
what we ought to be
without being one with God
and having the same will as the Most High.
Separated from God, we are like withered branches
which are thrown into the fire
and whose ashes are scattered by the winds.

To trust in God
is to share God's own life,
it is to feel in our soul the springtime
of an eternal becoming,
and it is to catch the rain of our years
like a flow of blessings
changing our weariness
into glory.

It is to share all the life of the universe,
to penetrate into what was
and what will be,
in what is near us
or far away;
it is to suffer all the transformations

of spirit
and flesh
but, to feel, nevertheless,
that we are always
the same entity
in a never-ceasing becoming
and elevation.

It is a dangerous and daring
pilgrimage,
like throwing oneself
into an abyss,
or an ascension toward the stars!
And what wonderful marvels
we find
when we take you,
O Christ,
as our Companion and Guide—
you, the Supreme Pioneer of our faith!

Buenos Aires, Argentina, 1978

My Old Age

I was a child
who ardently wanted to be a youth.
I was a youth
bursting with life
with dreams and daring undertakings.
I did achieve some,
others failed.
Not all that we crave in life is fulfilled;
what can be achieved, we have to do
with beauty, honesty, love.
My mature age passed by
with its risks, failures,
new attempts and new conquests;
now my old age has caught me,
with the weight of years
and remembrances,
and the conscience of still being
far from the goal set by God.
But, I do not regret
having become an old person.
I have lived my life, struggled, loved,
and the best of all is
that within me remains
the hope that not everything will end
in ashes and dust;
and though much of what I have done may have perished
and much may yet perish,
the love with which I loved
will continue to live
and flourish in other lives
as well as in my spirit
through paths of eternity.

Porto Alegre, Brazil, 1978

4.

Prose

The Social Action of the Church
The Boundaries of Religion

THERE ARE people who maintain that religion should have certain and definite limits: of time, of action, of influence. One can be religious at some periods in one's life, in certain sectors of human activity, in specified social spheres.

Others maintain that religion is an appendix, something which may be added to life, but which is not really necessary to life. It is a custom, a habit. Many times it is a hindrance, an obstacle to full human activity. Religion is confused with superstition.

There are others who make every possible effort to encourage people to divorce themselves from everything which attaches them to the "world," almost converting themselves into strangers in their social surroundings. A believer should be thinking of heaven, waiting for heaven, longing for heaven. Earth is a wicked place, completely under the influence of evil. Those who love God are bound to hate the earth, which with its apparent enchantments tries to deceive people in order to lure them to damnation.

It is the sublimation of egoism. It is the sanctification of individualism.

All these and similar conceptions spring from an erroneous point of view concerning the nature and function of religion in life.

The history of religion tells us that humanity, in every period of history and in all places, has been incurably religious. Every human being is born with the possibility of becoming religious. Human nature is so constituted that if one were born without a religious vocation, one would be abnormal. And, in a certain way, anyone is abnormal who does not develop the characteristics which tend to integrate life. Abundant life is the whole life. And there is no whole life without religion. Religion in life has the same function as the perfume in a flower. It is an element in life which infuses the environment with divine fragrance. It is like salt in food, like light in darkness. Life without religion becomes a tasteless existence, a burned-out lamp.

A person does not come to life alone, nor can a person live alone. We are social beings. And, as social beings, we cannot escape our duty of solidarity, our social obligation, our direct contribution to society, out of which we come. Through society we live and sustain ourselves. In the midst of society, willing or not, we have to undergo our earthly journey. To deny the help we receive is to show ingratitude; what humanity is today, with its defects and virtues, it owes to inheritance, which, through society, comes to it from generation to generation.

Also abnormal is the person who wants to pass through society and the world as one who does not have any duty towards it. The integrated persons in religion, especially in the Christian religion, are the ones who, striving towards divine perfection, try in the daily struggle to ameliorate their social surroundings. Really the "individual" and the "social" do not exist separately. The persons who try to live by and for the self only, end their course in annihilation. They would prove Jesus' rule: "Whoever would save his life will lose it" (Mark 8:35).

We do not find at the beginning of Christianity, of Christ's Christianity, a separation between the individual person and society. Jesus lived in society, trying to reform, or rather to inspire, with his ideals, life around him. The earth for him also is one of God's abodes, because where God is, there heaven is also. The prayer of the Master for his disciples, if we remember, was for God not to take his disciples from the world, but to deliver them from evil, and the commandment which he likened to the greatest of all commandments—the one which enjoins us to love God—is the one which requires us to love our neighbors. And we cannot love our neighbors by separating ourselves from them. We must live, struggle, and triumph with them.

It is reasonable that we, as Christians, should not cooperate with enterprises or movements which are destined to work for evil. But in all that may be betterment, elevation of purpose, progress, we must cooperate in a free, spontaneous, and happy spirit. The kingdom of God will not be established on earth just because we pray for it in the Lord's prayer. The kingdom of God will come when men and women of goodwill, possessed by the Holy Spirit, Christ's spirit, feel more fervently their social responsibility and seek to practice in society the idealistic principles of the Master. For religion there should be no limits. We should live always, wherever we may find ourselves, within its atmosphere—seven days a week, twenty-four hours a day. This is the limit of time for true religion. Only a religion of this kind can have influence and be a fountain of power for the attainment of *abundant life*.

The Teachings of Jesus
Chapter IX: The Family

Excerpt: The Mission of the Mother in the Home

THE IDEALS, that we want the society of tomorrow to have, should be sown little by little by mothers in their homes. The mother is not only the mistress of the house; she is, above all else, an educator. She should be the best teacher of religious education for her children. If faith is to return to men and women it will be only through Christian mothers, who, while they are nursing their children, can also teach them that there is only one God and Father, who nourishes the life of the whole universe and who loves all of us. If fraternity is to return to humankind, it will be through the patient lessons of the mother, who will tell the little ones that this world belongs to all God's children, whether they are white or black, rich or poor, big or small. If war is going to end someday, it will be through the loving work of mothers who, thinking about other mothers beyond their frontiers who are also nursing little ones, will teach their children to love, not hate, their neighbors; it will be through mothers who will not give their children toy soldiers and weapons, but instead will tell them the wonderful story of the great benefactors of humanity, persons who through study and love worked to transform this world into a better and beautiful one.

If purity is to return to the world, it will be only through mothers who will teach their children the value of true honesty; who will also hold up as an example to them the child Jesus, who, when he was twelve years old, conversed with the sages of the law seeking to know more about God and justice, and who when he became a man, chose to die on a cross, in order to save us from evil, rather than to yield to sin.

The Teachings of Jesus
Chapter X: The State

Fragment

4. What Is the Relation between the State and God's Kingdom?

JESUS said that we should "render therefore to Caesar the things that are Caesar's, and to God the things that are God's (Matt. 22:21). But there are occasions when, in order to give what Caesar demands, we would be forced to give him what belongs to God. For a Christian, conscious of human duties there is no human compulsion which should oblige him to deny God's supremacy. Is it lack of patriotism? Some people label it so, only because they may not agree with the governing majority. Even Jesus was accused of a lack of patriotism. Paul was persecuted by his countrymen, who tried several times to take his life. Peter and John preferred to be punished by the authorities rather than to obey the order not to talk in Jesus' name, adducing that it was more important to listen to God than to them (Acts 4:19).

But these are exceptions. In normal times, Christians should not deny the state their cooperation. But they should remember, however, the principle established by the Master: "Let the greatest among you become as the youngest, and the leader as one who serves" (Luke 22:26). With this as their purpose and having the opportunity to serve the state, they will discharge their duty. This means that the state will not change, while the feelings of the people leading it do not change. A passive attitude on the part of the believer, is not right or good. In relation to the state, we have to be "salt" and "light." It will not be a position of privilege, but of service.

For this reason Christians should exercise their right to vote, supporting the most honorable citizens from whom they expect the greatest commitment to the common good and progress for all. They should not feel obligated to vote for one name or many, only because that one is sponsored by this or that party against the candidates of other parties. It is also immoral that Christians vote for those whom they know will not defend the interests of the nation, only because the person is a member of their party. Their country should stand above their party. Believers in Christ should keep their conscience free to vote for whomever they wish and not feel compelled to accept any candidate. And if they do not proceed in this fashion, taking into consideration the well-being of the people, they will, as has frequently occurred, vote for Barrabas and disown Jesus.

On a certain occasion John the Baptist sent a delegation of his disciples to Jesus, to find out if he was really God's messiah. After the envoys had left, Jesus paid homage to John. He said, among other things: "What did you go out into the wilderness to behold? A reed shaken by the wind? What then did you go out to see? A man clothed in soft clothing? Behold, those who are gorgeously appareled and live in luxury are in kings' courts. What then did you go out to see? A prophet? Yes, I tell you, and more than a prophet. This is he of whom it is written, 'Behold, I send my messenger before thy face, who shall prepare thy way before thee.' I tell you, among those born of women none is greater than John; yet he who is least in the kingdom of God is greater than he" (Luke 7:24-28).

In this passage we have one of the most valuable teachings about our present subject.

a. To Rule Is Not a Frivolous Matter.

We notice that the popular concept is that life in high places is one of luxury. There we find people splendidly dressed. They do not have working garments, but the clothes of those who are ready for a banquet. The way in which Jesus expresses himself is ironic, one of reprobation. Generally, though, this was the idea people had of government: a role of privileges in order to enjoy an easier life. On the other hand, in considering the responsibility that a state has, it would be proper that those in charge should give more serious consideration to their conduct. The state does not have to deal with matters of secondary importance: what is in its hands is the destiny of millions of lives. If there are frivolous ideas about government, they should be shunned. Nobody should think that life is just a celebration, certainly not the men and women leading a state.

b. Those Who Rule Do Not Have the Right to an Immoral Life.

We should remember that John the Baptist was imprisoned for denouncing the immoral life of Herod the tetrarch of Galilee and Perea. The prophet did not hesitate to reprove iniquity even if it was found in royal palaces. His strong voice was raised, in a harsh and firm tone, against the evil that was being entrenched in might and power. Jesus approves of John's conduct. He points to him as the greatest of the prophets. For Jesus, just as for John, abuse was abuse even within the royal palaces. Statesmen do not have the right to commit immoral acts just because they are statesmen. Because they hold such a position is precisely why their responsibility is greater: being at the head of the people, they are bound to be examples of virtue and honesty.

c. To Belong to the Kingdom Is More Than to Belong to Any Government.

We have to emphasize the importance that Jesus gave to the kingdom of God. Those who belong to this kingdom are even greater than the greatest of people outside it. There is no other post, no other position which is more honorable than to be a disciple of Jesus. This should be taken as a norm by those who, having been elevated to posts in government, undervalue their Christian merits. Even in the highest post of the State, those who deny they are Christians, or are ashamed of it, like Esau, are selling their birthright for a pottage of lentils. There is no human honor which is equivalent to the honor of belonging to a kingdom where justice and love reign forever. The duty of the leaders who consider themselves members of the kingdom of God, is not that of hiding their friendship with Jesus, but of practicing before the world the principles which in the end will determine the final triumph of the cause of God among people. In this way they will make their state a reflection of the rule of God in the world, and will hasten its coming to us.

Wanderings of My Spirit

Sunflowers

IT IS two o'clock in the afternoon, in a late summer on the Uruguayan prairie. It is not possible to take a *siesta,* when from the outside one hears the wind weeping through the boughs of the pine and the eucalyptus trees. It is like an infinite groaning, an unceasing singing, as if it were the restless spirit of invisible things in search of realization.

No, the Pilgrim cannot sleep. He feels within himself something like a poetical wind soaking, shaking, exciting him. And, to the fluttering of the waves of the air, he adds the votive sigh of a dream of beauty and truth.

To be in the open air, to feel the very blood of nature flowing in his own veins, what a venture! It is the tonic and respite against the stress to which human beings are subjected in the treacherous and multifarious city.

Why did we build for ourselves such huge cities, where it seems that spirits are in prison and bodies in shackles? It was, certainly, the city which led us to be lords and exploiters of our fellow beings, because, outside, at the sound of the wind, and under the light of the free and fecundating sun, the human spirit aspires to fly and to love!

It is because among the fields the very spirit of liberty lives and vibrates.

Under the trees the Pilgrim went on that Sunday afternoon of that dying summer. And the wind, through the darker green of the leaves, was singing rhymes which he felt vibrating in the tissue of his soul. And the boughs, in the waving of the wind, seemed to come to him as if to embrace him with a friendly and affectionate hug: the embrace of Mother Nature to the prodigal son, who, thirsty for peace and sweetness was returning from the city to her bosom!

Under the sun went the Pilgrim desiring to contemplate the

fields. And in front of him a large, vast extension of gold-like color was glittering, a moving extension which was combining itself yonder, with the blue of the horizon; it was a field of sunflowers. The wind which was blowing, with its strong impetus, was bending the haughty necks of the sunflowers towards the ground. But when the wind would temporarily cease to blow, so as to double its impetuosity, the sunflowers would lift again their faces toward the sun, searching for its caressing and warm kiss.

And that field of sunflowers, insistent on looking to the sun, was transformed, in the Pilgrim's mind, into an immense multitude of people who wished to look at the truth, but were forced to look at the black and arid earth: a multitude who wanted light but on whom darkness was enforced.

Yes, that was the symbol of humanity who wants the sun of the abundant and peaceful life, and who receives in her heart the blast of doubt and death.

"Life! Life! I want life, healthy and beautiful life!" man, in the prime of his existence, demands. But war in the battlefields of Europe and Asia is sowing desolation. He saw figures of young men, who want the sun of life, but receive in their dreaming heads shots of death!

God, my God!

And the struggle between the wind, the sun, the sunflowers, in the golden afternoon, is going on. Struggle of beauty and vision of grief!

But in the prairie of the Pilgrim's soul, under the pine trees, another wind is blowing. It is the wind of God's spirit. It is the voice of hope. It is the voice of faith. It is the energy of love. And the Pilgrim hears another melody: it is a melody which does not come from the trees, or from the sunflowers.

"And I, when I am lifted up from the earth, will draw all men to myself."

And the Pilgrim's soul asks: "Have you not been lifted up? Have you not been crucified? Were you not our sun? Why are not men looking at you as the sunflowers in the field look at the sun?"

And the voice of the Spirit speaks again in his conscience: "Go and preach the gospel to every creature."

Yes, it is true that not all know as yet that Christ is the sun, the life.

How many are there who do not know? How many?

Thousands?

Millions!

Almost twenty centuries of Christian history!

And there is still so much to be done! So much!

And when will the kingdom of evil have its end?

It will not come until "at the name of Jesus every knee should bow, in heaven and on earth and under the earth, and every tongue confess that Jesus Christ is Lord, to the glory of God the father" (Phil. 2:10).

And the Pilgrim looked at the field of sunflowers and he remembered the big city, with its thousands and millions of men and women who looked at the ground and could not see the light.

And he understood that it was necessary to leave behind the music of the wind and go back to the city to catch the sobs of the multitudes, till all eyes, full of smiles and hopes, may look at the sun of life, and every ear may hear the eternal music of the heavenly spheres.

Montevideo, Uruguay
March 4, 1940

How Much Value Has a Human Being?

HOW MUCH value has a human being in this world of ours?

If I read the ancient thought of the Psalmist, I find that a human being is valued ''little less than God'' (Psalm 8:5).

If I read the newspapers I discover that human beings are worth less than the animals of the fields.

Jesus already asked: ''Of how much more value is a man than a sheep!'' (Matt. 12:12). Why did he ask that question? Simply because he noticed that even the religion of his country showed more consideration, on the sabbath day, for a sheep which had fallen into a pit, than for a sick person.

In reality how much value has a human being?

Ask the mother who gave him life. She will tell you how much care, fear, sacrifice, tears, anxiety, time, endurance, and love are required to shape just one human being.

Ask a general. For him he will be of little value; he will be lost in the great plans of his conquests—just an insignificant number in the sum total of victims destined for immolation; never a person with aspirations, desires, and feelings; always an automaton without his own will; never a being conscious of his rights and duties, and master of his life and liberty; always a victim who has to die without asking why, where, and when; without the right to inquire about his destiny or to claim his affections. He is a thing, a numerical expression, a heap of abandoned bones at the edge of roads, in the furrows of devastated fields. . . .

There will be mothers who will provide other sons to the ''Fatherland,'' to fill in the spaces left today in the endless lines of the victims of unknown objectives engendered by blind and rush egoism.

Of how much value is a human being?

Ask a physician who is conscious of his humanitarian duties, or a sage who is dedicated to his sacred mission.

You will find him consulting his books, meditating or looking through the telescope, seeking to penetrate the mysteries of life and death, devoting himself to the discovery of a means to extend, even for one more day, a life, or for another hour, the tranquility or happiness of a fellow being. And then multiply the sages by the thousands and for generations of generations, put together their findings and their anxieties, their struggles and martyrdoms, and you will have an idea of what is for them the value of a human life.

What is the value of a human life?
Ask the big commercial and industrial concerns. They will talk to you about figures, dividends, of profits and losses, of markets and raw materials. . . . but about human beings, the basis of their capital, they will know very little.
What do they know about those workmen who wet with the sweat of their faces the work of their hands? What do they know about their needs? Will one of them consider that those human beings, who go in and out of the doors of their factories, do have hearts, souls, bodies as they do?
Will they be conscious of the rights of their workmen? It may be that the children of those fathers and mothers who work for them, and who roam through the streets and squares, without a place in the schools, and the joy of a real home, may be able to give an answer. They are a poor testimony of what the life of a human being is worth. And also those infested shacks in the poor abandoned neighborhoods, where so much misery and anguish are concentrated!

How much value has a human being?
For his sweat and blood, he will get from his employers just enough for them to choke before the tribunal of history the voice of justice.

How much is a human being worth?
Ask Francis of Assisi.
Ask the one who embraced and kissed the wretched lepers on

the crossroads of the sunny regions of Italy; ask him who loved so much the flowers and the birds. He will answer with the immortal testimony of his life—brief but marvelous—of his life which was not his, but offered in love and service to all his neighbors. He will tell you that a human being is worth more than the whole material world, that here is nothing, no, nothing which may pay the value of a human being.

He was called the "fool" of Assisi!

Blessed, divine "fool"! You knew, indeed, the mystery of the gospel of human redemption. In those hands of yours, into which sunk the stigma of the wounds of Christ's hands, you carried the romance of the love written with the hot iron of supreme zeal. The purifying flame, which would burn the cobwebs which had covered the human conscience, was burning in your bosom, so that the sons of men could once again look into the face of God.

All these thoughts and others were passing through my mind, when this morning I was meditating on the words which someone seated at my side in the tramway, reading the news of this last world war, said to me:

"Have you noticed how the wires, reporting the war actions, mention the number of aircraft destroyed, but never the young men who crashed with them?"

And this made me also see Jesus, leaving the distant synagogues of Galilee coming to us asking: "How much more value has a young life than an aircraft?"

And his question, uttered in my mind, revealed a tone of anxious sadness in his voice, and his looks were like those of one who carried a thorn in his heart.

Buenos Aires, Argentina
July 12, 1941

The Supereminence of Jesus
The Superiority of Jesus over Moses

"Yet Jesus has been counted worthy of as much more glory than Moses as the builder of a house has more honor than the house."

—Hebrews 3:3

AMONG the Jews, Moses was the most impressive figure in the history of Israel. He was the giant man, who, with extraordinary power, had liberated an entire population from slavery to lead them, through a desert, to a land of freedom, to a land which, according to the biblical saying, was flowing with "milk and honey." Moses had also gained the respect of the Israelites, acquiring their confidence and admiration, because of the laws which he had left them as an inheritance, laws believed to be of changeless and eternal value.

We know that in Hebrew literature, law occupied first place, and it was venerated to such an extent that some scribes, through an excess of imagination, were led to assert that Jehovah, on the sabbath day applied himself to the study of law. For them the law given by Moses was the greatest revelation which God could reveal to humankind. For this reason a declaration like the one which we find in the letter to the Hebrews could appear tremendously daring and even blasphemous to the ears of those who were used to considering Moses the supreme arbiter of religious life. That declaration of Hebrews, notwithstanding, was in accord with what Jesus stated in his sermon on the Mount when he quotes certain parts of the ancient law and says: "You have heard that it was said to the men of old . . . , but I say to you . . . " (Matt. 5:21) How did Jesus and the writer of Hebrews go so far? Let us consider, though briefy, both personalities: Moses and Jesus.

1. Looking even superficially at Jesus' life and that of Moses we are convinced of the moral and spiritual superiority of our master, and here is proven to be true the saying according to

which not always the one who lives for more years gives greater significance to his life, because the most significant life may comprise a very limited space of time. Methuselah lived almost one thousand years, and according to the biblical record he was the man who lived more than any other; but his long age is the only thing we remember about him. Jesus lived a little more than a fourth of the life of Moses; nevertheless, his life surpasses tremendously the life of the great legislator.

Moses has stains of blood in his life, impulses of wrath and revenge. In Jesus we always find evident the genius of the person who loves innocence, who excels by his goodness and tolerance, and who triumphs with forgiveness. We admire in Moses the patience he endured with his people, for a long period of time. Despite his greatness, he merges with the people whom he leads and from whom he originated.

Jesus never stained his hands with the blood of his brethren. The only blood which stained his path was his own blood, offered as a living sacrifice for those whom he loved and also for those who crucified him. In the life of Moses, when we look into the depth of his nature, we find the man; in the life of Jesus, when we penetrate his intimate being, we find the very image of God.

2. Moses was a legislator. He provided laws which tried to minister to the necessities of the entire life of his people. He gave special direction to life, bringing them out of slavery and leading them to a state of liberty. But, laws always have, regardless of the halo which we attach to them, the quality of transient values.

What is bad about laws is that we invest them with immutableness, and they then turn from servants into masters. This was what happened with the laws of "the God of Israel," written in the distant past. Applied to needs of other times, they were still operating in Jesus' time, so that man was their slave.

Jesus did not come with laws, though many have conceived of him as the legislator of a new covenant, and the giver of laws for the new dispensation. Jesus offered to men only principles, principles which have their origin in the inspiration of the Holy Spirit of God, principles which are basic, but which provide the elasticity which is required by the changes which every age brings. In a certain sense, law exists mainly to prohibit, it is the empire of "you shall not"; on the other hand, Jesus' principles are basic and they ordain: "you shall do." The first one denies, the second, affirms; the first one limits, the second is limitless; the first one imprisons the spirit, the second provides wings.

3. Moses will be remembered in history as the liberator of a people and the forger of a nationality. It was due to his genius, his fortitude and his will—under God's power—that the people of Israel owe their liberty and their organization as an autonomous group. Moses was the man who taught the Israelites that it is preferable to die of hunger in the desert than to live in any other condition under the prepotent hand of a dictator; and under his direction the Israelites learned forever the song of liberty; though they were dominated several times by other nations, they never lost their vocation for liberty and never permitted their spirit and genius to be muzzled.

Jesus, on the other hand, not having been the liberator of a people and having refused to become a terrestrial king, was in a more ample sense, the liberator of all peoples. Jesus is not the defender of one race. In fact, he eliminates the separation that exists among races. For him fatherlands do not exist; for him there is only one fatherland: the whole world, of which God is the creator and all those who live in it are brothers.

Jesus' salvation does not consider the geographical limits imposed by the conventionality of human egoism. Jesus' liberty has its origin in God's universal spirit and it extends throughout the whole universe in search of every human being, who has lost the way and needs a guiding light. Moses could be venerated by the Israelites, but Jesus is worshipped by all peoples, because he has been felt everywhere, because he is not the Jew who kills the Egyptian to save the honor of his tribal blood, but the brother of all men and women trying to bring peace to all hearts. The difference at this point between Jesus and Moses is that which exists between an alley which ends in an insurmountable wall and a wide avenue which extends toward the immensity of the horizon.

4. Moses projects himself into the minds of people as the

inexorable judge who demands obedience. Human beings obey or die by the curse of their sin. In Jesus we find the friend, the one who opens his arms to the whole of humankind, saying: "Come unto me, come unto me, because I am the way to true life." He comes to us as a love poem of God given as vivifying grace. He teaches men and women not to obey, because disobedience would require punishment, but he invites them to love and to act in love, because the God in his nature is love. In front of Moses a sword is suspended, in front of Jesus there is a cross which invites. The sword makes a human being an obedient and submissive slave, the cross makes a human being a free and victorious spirit.

We do not want to give the impression that we are diminishing the value of Moses. Within his age, within his understanding of values, within the limits of his mind, facing the moral littleness of his contemporaries, Moses is an imposing figure. Nevertheless compared to Jesus, his personality diminishes and that of Jesus increases. And, surely, if we could be found with Moses at Jesus' feet, he would tell us what John the Baptist said to his disciples when Jesus was plainly revealed to him, "He must increase, but I must decrease" (John 3:30).

Meditations of My Path
In the Shade of the Eucalyptus Trees

SUMPTUOUS residence in the shade of the eucalyptus trees, in the undulating plains of South Rio Grande in Brasil. Flowerbeds all around, vivid green lawns . . . the wind was performing on the keyboard of the tree leaves the romantic melody of the wide open prairies!

Peace . . . Poetry . . . A spot for rhapsody, dreams. . . .
We thought: "Who lives here, so lucky?"
We knocked.

117

At the door an elegant lady, richly dressed, received us. She had the air of an aristocratic lady, accustomed to comfort and to the whims of an easy life. Her husband, whom we were looking for, was not there at the moment—he might return in a few moments, we could wait for him.

She invited us to the lavish parlor: books with golden backs scattered on small tables, in the corners . . . fine carpets covering the floor . . . richly dressed chairs . . . glittering electric-light fixtures . . . luxury, comfort, everything that vanity desires.

We were waiting . . .

Meanwhile the lady was entertaining us with her conversation. She told us about her trips to Europe, Australia, and North America, about her husband's business, about markets. But in her face of a rich woman there was a sadness. A satiety of everything was evident in her. Her eyes revealed an unbearable boredom.

And afterwards, in a bitter tone—confession of the moral failure of egoistic materialism—she said, "Life here is so insipid, monotonous, unvarying . . . I am so tired of this place . . . The days are too long in this solitude. I do not know what to do with time, with my life . . ."

And she sighed, a deep, long sigh . . .

Those words sent shivers up my spine. And that conversation painfully penetrated my inner spirit. And with the insistence of a dripping faucet, the words: "I am tired . . . I do not know what to do with my life!" troubled me the whole afternoon.

Not to know what to do in a world so full of needs?

There, a short distance from that mansion, one could see the wretched shacks, with their wide crevices through which the wind entered, with their low roofs of rusted metal . . . badly nourished children, suffering women, bending under the weight of unhealthy and badly paid work . . . old cots, inconveniences, a lack of everything! . . .

Nothing to do in this life? No!

What there was in that existence was the lack of an ideal, the absence of a social conscience, the blunting of the esthetic sentiment of life.

118

There was a lack of love which redeems, of the vision which sublimates, of the light which pierces darkness.

Afterwards, in the silence of the following night, I heard a voice—Paul's voice, the daring pilgrim of the gospel—speaking to me of someone:

"For you know the grace of our Lord Jesus Christ, that though he was rich, yet for your sake he became poor so that by his poverty you might become rich" (2 Cor. 8-9).

And, to his voice, the great voice of the centuries echoed:

"Truly, truly, I say to you, unless a grain of wheat falls into the earth and dies, it remains alone; but if it dies, it bears much fruit. He who loves his life loses it" (John 12:24-25).

And in the silence of my room, it seemed to me that I could hear the wind blowing through the faraway eucalyptus trees, reciting a weeping psalm and scattering its sobs over a lost life, in a beautiful mansion . . .

Porto Alegre
September, 1937

Neither Lords Nor Slaves

ACT II   SCENE I

Priscilla

(Priscilla is in the room where Paul and Aquila have finished the tent for Philemon. She is looking through the window and contemplates the scenery outside. Then says:)

There I see the blue sea. How bright and serene it is under the first rays of the day! Truly the great singer of our people was right when he did sing on his lyre:

119

The heavens are telling the glory of God;
and the firmament proclaims his handiwork.
Day to day pours forth speech,
and night to night declares knowledge.

*(A soft music coming from afar is heard imitating the
coming of dawn, Priscilla is silent for a moment, as if
she were meditating. She is interrupted by a knock at
the door. Quickly she goes to open the door and says:)*

Grace and peace in the Lord! You are welcome! Come in!

*(Two men come in, Philemon of Colossae who comes
forward with an arrogant stride and Onesimus, his
slave in humble manner, behind him. Philemon comes
finely dressed in a purple tunic and Onesimus is bare-
foot wearing a very dark rustic tunic.)*

Philemon

(Coming forward and gently bowing his head)

Peace be with you, good woman.

(Onesimus remains standing at the door speechless.)

Priscilla

(Offering seats to the visitors)

Aquila and Paul worked all night long so as to be able to finish
the tent that you requested, Philemon. I am going to call them.

(She goes out)

*(Philemon sits on the bench, Onesimus stays at a dis-
tance and sits down on the floor. He looks around with
a curious and diffident air.)*

Philemon

(As if he were speaking to himself)

These Christians are very strange, but very conscientious! There the tent is! It would not have been more expensive in some other place, but I am sure that it is well done and with select materials. It is a pity that workers of this kind have let themselves be influenced by the ideas of such strange gods. This hurts their business. I would like to persuade them to forget this foolishness and think seriously about their business, since they could accumulate a small fortune with it. I myself would be willing to take them with me to Colossas and to lend them money to expand their commercial opportunities, but there is no chance of that. They say that they work not to get rich, but only to have the means to support themselves and be able to propagate their ideas . . . What a way of being crazy! In life one has to live on realities and not on dreams . . .

(He pauses. He realizes that he is not alone when he looks at the door, where to one side on the floor Onesimus is sitting. He speaks then to Onesimus:)

Onesimus, by the way, did you hear all the commotion last night through the city? Do you know why they shouted so loudly in the streets in favor of our goddess Diana?

Onesimus

Yes, lord, not only did I hear it but I also saw it. I was coming back from the harbor where I had gone to take your message to the boatmen who should have left this morning for the islands of the Aegean when I met the crowd which was infuriated against the Christians. It was led by the silversmith Demetrius, the man who sold you a silver shrine of Artemis which you bought to take to your home in Colossas. He was shouting with his fellow workmen that the Christians were trying to defame the greatness and the power of the goddess.

121

Philemon

What a way for these Christians to risk their lives, just for pure talkativeness, when they could live in peace . . . For me the best philosophy is that which says: 'Let us drink and eat because tomorrow we shall die . . .'

Onesimus

It may be that you are right, my lord. But, what about those who have neither food, nor drink, nor liberty? And in this world there are so many! And, more than once, I have heard this Paul, the tent-maker, speak at the public market to groups of slaves like me, as if we were his brothers. He spoke to us of a God who, according to him, is the only one who exists. He also told us that he is the father of all men, affirming that he 'made from one every nation of men to live on the face of the earth' and that it is not necessary to look for him in far away places since he is not far from any of us. He said, also, that this God manifested himself in flesh in Palestine, among the Jews in the person of a certain Jesus, who had been a carpenter, and whom the religious people of his land killed, putting him on a cross. But this God, father of all men, made him live again. Paul states that this Jesus manifested himself to him after he had risen. And he says that this carpenter came encarnating God, to make of all men just one family and of the world just one kingdom. What was most marvelous to me was that he said that also we, the slaves, can participate and have equal rights in that kingdom. Indeed I remember that he stressed the following words: 'In him there is neither Jew nor Greek, there is neither slave nor freeman, there is neither male nor female, for you are all one in Christ Jesus . . .' This philosophy appeals to me, since I believed that I was born to always be a slave and nothing more than a slave.

Philemon

This is true, Onesimus. You were born a slave and you will always be a slave. Of this there is no doubt. Do not let yourself be fooled and your judgment be poisoned by perverted and queer doctrines. These Christians want to know more than our philosophers. Did not Aristotle himself, disciple of the great Plato, who in his turn was the disciple of Socrates, affirm that there are men that by their own nature are slaves and others lords? How do these poor visionaries and dreamers want to change the action and determination of nature? This is foolishness, crazy words! Do not pay any attention to them! Be satisfied by always being a good servant, obedient and submissive as you have been up to now . . . You will never be without bread, or a roof . . . I prohibit you to continue listening to these perverters of consciences, to these preachers of false doctrines, to these destroyers of the faith of our fathers . . .

Onesimus

But, my lord, to me their words seemed very reasonable! I already felt I was somebody in the world and in my life; something more than an instrument of work as an oxen or a horse, (beating his breast). I already felt that I had a soul within my chest; and with an eternal soul; and with a father who takes care of me in heaven . . . These words of the tent-maker Paul will never leave my ears: ". . . in him there is neither lord, nor slave . . ."

Philemon

Shut up, shut up . . . It seems to me that these talks are corrupting your good judgement! What! Do you want to have the same right that I have in my life and in the world? Never! You were born a slave; a slave you will die. I was born a lord; your lord; and your lord I shall always be! I, (with vehemence) I am your father and nobody else! Don't you eat the bread from my ranch, are you not living under the roof of my property? . . .

Onesimus

But (he gets up) I need more than crumbs of bread and a rag to cover myself, and a mat to sleep on. I have a soul redeemed by

Jesus, I want to be a freeman like you. Paul has said: "All men were made of one blood . . ." (Acts 17:20, my paraphrase).

Philemon

(he gets up)

Shut up, renegade, heretic, thankless brute of the earth! I shall teach you when we get home, how many rights of freemen you have . . . There you will feel how much this rebellion and audacity will cost you! To tell me that you are worth as much as I! To dare to think that your vile blood is blood as noble as mine! Insolent, impertinent worm, get out of my sight.

(He takes him by his arm and throws him out into the street and speaks to him from the door.)

Wait for me at the stage post and tell your companions Hermes and Nerus to come here with the beasts to pick up the tent. Go fast! and that I may not hear again a word of all this stupid pretension of yours!

Onesimus

(leaving the place and from outside)

The world of tomorrow will be a world without slaves.

Spiritual Currents in Spanish America
The Spirit of the Spanish Conquest

WHAT was really the spirit of the Spanish Conquest?

There is no doubt that from the beginning three exponents of the conquest were allies throughout the colonial period: the warrior-conqueror (destined to become the nucleus of the future military system), the friar or the priest, and the public official. They form the backbone of the new social order developing in America. The warrior-conqueror is the adventurer who, in the name of the king of Spain, seeks a new kingdom for his lord, with no other consideration than to acquire the largest amount of booty for himself and the crown.

The friar sets out, commissioned by both the king and the Pope, to subdue, in the name of the "Holy Catholic Faith," the new vassals, whose human status is in question. The sword usually has as its ally the cross, which speaks of chastisement and hell to those who will not submit passively to the new faith.

The public official looks after the business of his king, trying to send to Spain the largest possible amount of material goods, and taking advantage of the position he holds for his own personal benefit. He tries at the same time to maintain a wall of partition between the conqueror and the friar, sometimes difficult, indeed almost impossible to do. He endeavors also to apply the laws of the Indies, forged in Spain to the little-known situations and needs in America, laws which were in many cases very humanitarian, but impracticable out in the field.

There is no doubt that the profit motive looms large in the conquest. Even if the priest or the friar comes mainly to minister to the spiritual needs, of both the conqueror and the conquered, the enterprise is carried out in such a way as to get material benefit out of it.

However, Spain contributed some permanent characteristics to our Spanish American countries. She gave them a common language, even though there are many millions who speak mainly or only their aboriginal tongues. This common language is a very important factor. One can travel from one country to another without the necessity of speaking a new tongue. There are, of course, some slight variations in the use of words, and in their pronunciation.

But this is negligible. This common heritage brings about a constant interchange of thoughts and experiences, and there is a constant flow of books, magazines and newspapers from country to country.

If one knows Spanish, Portuguese, and English, he or she can go, with very few exceptions, anywhere in the whole of America and will feel at home. One will not need an interpreter, except among the Indians who live in communities by themselves. This is a marvelous thing which is not found in such an extensive area anywhere else on our globe.

Then, if we do not take into account the aboriginal elements, Spain provided a common human substratum. Spanish America, no matter how many immigrants she may receive, will remain Spanish in her culture and in her mode of expression. There will be modifications here and there, but in the main, all American countries are conscious of their common heritage and common destiny. There have been rivalries and wars among them, but they have not been bitter or race-conscious, as in other parts of the world. These are a mere remnant of the rebellious and jealous spirit which we discover in the conquerors of former days, who one day marched together in their conquests, and the next attacked each other as mortal enemies. There is a willingness now among them to enter into more intimate and effective collaboration and understanding, though at times it is barely evident. In Spanish America and Brazil there is no deep racial prejudice. It exists in some places, but it does not constitute an acute problem. There are people who are considered inferior on account of their limited culture and backward traditions. But on the whole there is nowhere clear-cut racial prejudice.

The chivalrous spirit of the conquerors and their deep-seated ambitions were responsible for opening up great trails in the immense distances of the continent. They were never satisfied to stay where they had pitched their tents. They were always seeking new deposits of gold just beyond them.

A chivalrous and adventurous spirit is not bad in itself, but must be guided in order to benefit both the individual and the group in general. The fighting spirit must be ennobled; we have to fight against the evil things in life and society. The Spaniards sowed the nomadic spirit of Don Quixote, but not the disinterested and pure-hearted purpose of the great hero-dreamer. This is the element which is lacking. It is necessary to go somewhere, to fight, to struggle, to conquer. But for what and how? That is the great question.

A new conquest of America must be made. But not with the sword, nor with bigotry and intolerance. Christ must reappear with the new conquerors, but without the sword and the thirst for gold. He must come with a gospel which redeems, a spirit that inspires and uplifts, a heart which can love everybody, and a sense of justice which can iron out all differences. He must assert more strongly the idea of a common origin and a common destiny, making our whole continent really a *new* continent, which will be able to contribute to the happiness of the whole world, exhibiting to all the fruits of a new way of life and a fresh and stimulating sense of real brotherhood. And in this sense, Protestantism has much to contribute directly or indirectly, which does not necessarily mean the exportation of all the traditions and anachronistic forms of theology, ecclesiasticism and denominationalism. What we need is the sowing of profound Christian concerns and the opening up of the vision of the real "El Dorado," the real Golden Realm, the kingdom of God, as it looms largely and graciously in the life, teaching and continuous passion of Christ, our Lord and Master.

Who Leads You?
To the Young People of the Church

Let no one despise your youth, but set the believers an example in speech and conduct, in love, in faith, in purity.

–1 Timothy 4:12

IT WOULD be an admirable thing if all the young people of the Church could awake to the reality of the present moment, could feel all the tremendous responsibility, and could be conscious of this enviable opportunity and would take advantage of their new spirited strength, putting it completely at God's disposition.

If all the youth of the Church, by unanimous consent, would put themselves at the disposition of Christ, they would constitute an irresistible force and a spiritual lever of extraordinary thrust. Undoubtedly, there is a good portion which is dedicating itself in one way or another to the task of the Church. But not all are. And all without exception should be willing to answer the urgent call of the master: ''Here I am.''

The whole world is a tremendous field of service. But the world does not need only service. This service requires a certain quality. The world requires service inspired by idealism.

How would we reconstruct the world? Much of what is being reconstructed, is reconstructed on a false base, with a cynical criterium of material instability. Egoism is violently destroying the inner world of humanity. It is good to remember that nothing permanent is constructed which does not have a firm inner basis—in the soul.

The world of tomorrow has to be a world impregnated with Christian idealism in order to endure; in this way it will be in harmony with God's will. Christian youth has to put itself in the front line, in order to struggle for the coming of a new order of things.

A groan of desperate anguish is issuing forth from the afflicted bowels of our world.

May no one remain insensitive in his place! May no one pretend not to hear the voice which is imploring! May no one deny his contribution to the great work of the establishment of the kingdom of God! May they all say: "Lord, we have heard thy voice, and we shall march!"

A Strange Lineage of Daring People
Stories of Methodist Pioneers

Introduction

HISTORY is the only link in our social life to the past. If we disregarded history, we would cut out an important section of our life. We can exist without history, but not live, because living is, in a certain way, reliving the history of our people, incarnating in us the yearnings which throbbed in the hearts and wills of people who are no more. In history life which came before takes refuge so as not to die altogether, but to spring up again, and to induce us to live. For this reason the Spanish thinker Miguel de Unamuno said, "It is the vision of the past which pushes us towards the conquest of the future, with the timber of recollections we fashion our hopes." When the present seems trivial and meaningless, lacking stimulation and inspiration, we need to look at the past, at history, so that we may feel "pushed towards the conquest of the future."

And we want to underscore this need of looking ahead "to the conquest of the future," because we should not be enthralled by the vision of the past, but receive the incentive to carry us to higher achievements and on to more daring adventures, so that the treasures of the past may be enriched by the events of the present. Knowledge of the past should not transform itself into chains, but into seed which can fertilize our minds and hearts, spirit and will, and give us the power to create beautiful, fresh, eternal works.

A Strange Lineage of Daring People
Chapter VIII: The One Who Wished to Have the Wings of an Eagle

DR. THOMAS COKE, not satisfied with his endless trips through England, Scotland, Ireland, Wales, North America, and the English Caribbean Islands, toward the end of his career was obsessed by the idea of starting missionary work in India. In 1813 he appeared before the sessions of the Annual Conference in England, beseeching his brethren to send him, along with other missionaries, to that distant point, with which he had been in touch through correspondence for many years. To the Annual Conference, his missionary plan to India seemed something preposterous and impossible to execute, especially due to the cost of the enterprise. Besides that, there was the opposition of those in England who maintained commercial interests in India and who did not want the influence of the Gospel to impair their business. At the same time some of his friends tried to dissuade him, on account of his age, from carrying out his project. He was sixty-six years old and his health was poor. To a friend who had written trying to convince him to abandon his plans he wrote:

> I am now dead to Europe, and alive for India. God himself has said to me, "Go to Ceylon!" I would rather be set naked on its coasts, without a friend, than not go. I am continually learning the Portuguese language.

When finally, the Annual Conference rejected his project, he went back to his lodging, crying despairingly. He spent almost the whole night in tears, praying. A missionary friend who had kept him company the night before, found his bed untouched the next morning. Truly, Dr. Coke, had not gone to bed and when he went back to the meeting hall he made a touching and pathetic appeal for the Conference to revoke its previous decision. He did again offer to go and also put at their disposition the sum of thirty thousand dollars to defray the expenses. Faced with this dramatic offer, which was defended by some friends, the Conference could not resist. It would have appeared to be in opposition to God's will! Finally, they voted to authorize him to go, and to take with him another seven companions one for South Africa, and the others for India. He went back to his lodging now weeping for joy and saying to the missionary who had accompanied him the night before: "Did I not tell you that God would answer our prayers?"

On December 30, 1813, Dr. Coke and the other missionaries departed for India. The trip was too long for the old, sick visionary. Many storms buffeted the vessel in which they were traveling, and on the morning of March 3, 1814, when they were already near their goal, the servant who called at his door at five thirty, the hour at which he always got up, did not receive an answer. Dr. Coke was lying on the floor with a smile still on his face. It seems that he got up to call for help, and died from a stroke.

The bosom of the waves received the body of the great missionary. The soldiers who were on board were standing beside his bier, while the bell was sadly ringing its farewell. All the passengers and the crew participated in pathetic silence in the ceremony of his burial, at the time when the sun was going down over the waters. Someone said that the body of such a great soul could only have for a grave a place as vast as the ocean. His work did not set with the setting of the light of that day.

Though his companions were shocked by his death, they went on with the enterprise. And they established in those faraway lands the seed of our faith, which through the years would produce permanent and abundant fruit. When the news of his death reached North America, the Annual Conference asked Bishop Francis Asbury to preach the sermon in his memory. His former colleague recorded in his diary:

> By vote of the Conference I preached the funeral sermon for Dr. Coke—of blessed mind and soul—of

131

the third branch of Oxonian Methodists—a gentle-
man, a scholar and a Bishop, to us—and a minister of
Christ, in zeal, in labours, and in services; the greatest
man in the last century. (From his Journal, Sunday,
June 21, 1815).

A greater tribute than the one given by Asbury we cannot give.
He was not only the most outstanding man of his time among
those whom God raised from the bosom of the Methodist move-
ment, but his personality is still challenging us not to stop our
drive toward "the ends of the earth," in response to the com-
mand of Christ. "Go into all the world and preach the gospel to
the whole creation" (Mark 16:15).

The Beloved Physician

Fragment

IT WAS GROWING mournfully dark on the seven hills of the
capital of the Empire and the lastest events had deeply shaken its
soul. The ashes of the big fire which destroyed a large portion of
the city, seemed to float in the sensibility of the citizenry. In the
Christian community grief was deep. They had been accused of
having caused the fire; many of its members paid with their lives
a crime of which they were innocent; others had gone to safer
places; but the majority remained, ready to give till the end
witness to their faith, certain that the Lord would sustain them
and would in due time, give them victory in their cause.

In the room, where the apostle Paul had been confined, the
Roman soldier, who kept watch on him, was not seen. Only one
man was collecting some scattered parchments on the table, and
some clothes hanging on the wall. Already the penumbra was
starting to invade the place. All of a sudden the street door

opened and another man, wearing a hood, silently came in. He immediately closed the door behind him.

"Who is there?" asked the man who was in the room.

"Luke, God be with you!" said the person who had come in.

"God save you, Christopher. God has sent you. Thanks be to heaven!"

And, deeply touched by a profound emotion, they embraced each other with tenderness. Afterwards, Luke, the beloved physician, free from the embrace, looked at him from head to foot, as a father looks, with inquisitive interest, at a son, from whom he has been separated for a long time. There was a moment of profound silence.

"Yes, it is you, Christopher, my beloved son. You are still the same young man, strong and fair."

"You were not still expecting me, father?"

"Yes, but I was about to leave this city. I cannot live in it any more. It is full of blood and crimes . . . This is a soulless city, from which the killers of liberty and justice have gone to all the regions of the earth."

"Father Luke, why are you so exasperated?"

"Do you not know what has happened?"

"Little, I have just arrived this morning from Ostia. I saw many people departing. Do you know? I met John Mark."

"And he did not tell you anything?"

"Yes, he told me a little. But I noticed that he was hiding something very serious, because he was not as expressive and jovial as when I saw him in Cyprus."

"Nobody who comes to Rome, keeps for long a smile on his lips and hope in his soul! Rome is no more the she-wolf which nurses abandoned creatures. It is a she-wolf which crushes the lives of those who fall under its claws. He did not say anything about brother Paul?"

"No. He only showed me the way to get here and he recommended that I not talk to anybody on the road and that I cover my face, and enter the city at dark."

"But, what did he talk about, then?"

"About a fire which burned part of the city and that the Christians were accused of being responsible for it, and about the persecution which had befallen them . . .''

"And nothing else?"

"No, nothing more."

"And he, where was he going?"

"He remained in Ostia. He told me that he had to stay there to be useful to the refugees who were waiting for vessels which could take them out of Italy. Afterwards he will come back to Rome. He sends you greetings and good wishes for a happy journey."

"Did he tell you, where I am going?"

"No, where are you going, Luke?'

"To Spain."

"Do you still intend to go there?"

"Yes, I so desire."

"And brother Paul?"

"Paul!" and his voice trembled in his throat. He looked fixedly at Christopher, then he lifted his eyes towards the window, through which a very pale light was coming in.

"Yes, Paul, where is he? I hoped to see him here. Was he not living here with you? Were you not taking care of him?"

"Yes, he was here. But now I can no longer take care of him. Now I have to go to Spain. And you will go with me. I have everything set to go."

"But, and Paul will not be going with us?"

"He was going. But now he cannot. We will go in his place."

"In his place? What happened? Where is he?"

"The fire of Rome took him too."

"How? Was he not here with you?"

"Yes, but my beloved Christopher, he was accused of being one of the leaders of the incendiaries, its instigator, as Caesar's enemy, the one who was conspiring against Caesar, so that Christ, the Jew, could reign . . ."

"That he reigns and will reign is certain. But, before that, the end of the world will come."

"That day may not be far away. We have to leave Rome. I do not want it to come while we are here. Before, we have to go to

Spain where Paul wanted so much to go; he was always speaking of it! It was like an obsession. Sometimes he would wake up during the night with that fixed idea and would ask me: 'Luke, is everything ready for our trip to Spain?' We shall comply with his plans, and we shall send the Churches the last letters that he wrote.''

"The last letters!''

"Yes, he will not write other letters, Christopher. The Roman sword cut the thread of his earthly life.''

"What are you saying, Father?''

"We shall not see brother Paul again on this earth. Like Stephen for whom he was one of the judges, he gave his life for the Gospel.''

Christopher at first remained silent; then he gave out a cry as if a dagger had pierced his heart. He fell on the floor and hid his face with his hands. A sob cut the penumbra.

"Be brave, Christopher, some day it will happen to us too. But you know that those who die with the Lord, do not die. They live forever.''

Christopher did not answer. In his mind, as if it were lightning, he recollected the long trip which he had made from Misia to Rome to see Paul and go with him to Spain. And now, the great Apostle was not there.

"Get up, son! A Christian needs to be strong. I understand your grief because that which fills my heart is also very great. Christ will do justice. His kingdom is already coming from the Orient. Now our tears are of no avail, except to show our cowardice. A Christian cannot be a coward. He must face death serenely and know how to smile. A Christian begins to taste God's glory only after this life, beyond the sepulcher.''

And, when he had said these words, he took Christopher in his arms and helped him to his feet, and again, he embraced him as a father affectionately touches a son who he sees in the throes of profound agony.

"You must be hungry and tired, Christopher. Sit down. I have some meat and bread, and some fruit. We shall eat a little and we shall leave under the cover of night. We shall go to a meeting in a cave on the banks of the Tiber. We shall say goodbye to our brethren. And we shall pray with them, asking the Lord to guide our steps to Spain.''

He had just said those words when the street door was abruptly opened. Instinctively Luke and Christopher placed themselves against the wall, to defend their backs and face the enemy. A voice called out:

"Luke!"

"God be with you, Julius," answered Luke. Why have you come?''

"I thought that you had already departed.''

"No, here I am, I am planning to go tomorrow.''

"Who is with you?''

"My son in the faith, Christopher, who arrived before nightfall from Ostia. He comes from Troas.''

"Why did he come to this accursed Rome at such a time?''

"He is going with me to Spain. Everything is ready. Did you bring me the itinerary?''

"No!''

"Why?''

"I shall be your guide.''

"You?''

"Yes. I, this afternoon, put my post of centurion in the hands of my boss. I cannot serve the emperor anymore. He has his hands too stained with innocent blood; now I will also become a Christian. And, with you I shall go to Spain.''

"God bless you, Julius!''

"Do you want to baptize me?''

"Tonight, at our farewell to our brethren on the banks of the Tiber.''

"There is no more time, Luke. They are also looking for you. We have to go right now, through the shadows. Here I brought water. Baptize me.''

It was almost impossible to see in the room. Their figures were almost invisible in the darkness.

"Kneel down, Julius. Hold the water, Christopher.'' Julius knelt.

"Do you believe that Jesus is your Lord and died for you to save you from your sins?"

"Yes, I believe."

"Will you be faithful till death?"

"Yes, I will."

"Then, in the name of the Father, the Son, and the Holy Spirit, receive the baptism of regeneration." And he poured on his head the water which Christopher handed to him.

"May God keep you faithful, and make you see his glory."

"Amen!" Christopher exclaimed.

"Amen!" added Julius. "And now, let's go! We cannot waste one minute. The soldiers will be here soon. Tonight there will be another search. Nero's thirst for blood is not yet satiated. He will have much to answer for on judgement day.

Hastily Luke searched for the bundles which he had put together and took some of them. Julius and Christopher took the rest. And the three men, shutting the door behind them, went furtively away.

Outside in the sky the stars were shining. Hooded, they slipped away through the shadows toward the Tiber, where the water seemed to express the agony of those who were groaning under Nero's crazy despotism. From afar an uproar of voices reached their ears. Torches, with flickering light, were breaking through the shadows. And a horrible cry reached the ears of the fugitives. "Death to the Christian! Death to the enemies of Caesar!" The three runaways hastened their steps. The water of the river covered the noise of their footsteps. Shortly they found themselves a safe distance away from the voices and the lights.

They crossed a field and found themselves on the road that would take them to the northern part of the peninsula. There were few people there. Nobody would have said that those three hooded figures were three Christians who were heading towards Spain, with the intention of preaching there the eternal triumph of the crucified one, whose name Nero was trying to erase from the minds of the Roman people.

You Shall Call His Name Jesus
Chapter VI: World Citizen

Fragment

DO WE HAVE, as Christians, a true conception of what it means to belong to God's kingdom? Sometimes it seems that we do not. We are subjected to the same temptation that the Church of Jerusalem was: that of confining ourselves within certain boundaries; of thinking that we can reach our salvation alone, without the help of other people; that we do not have other obligations except those which our own traditions and blood prescribe; that the social, political and religious structures of our country are the best in the world. When we come to belong to God's kingdom, through our conversion and allegiance to Jesus, we no longer have frontiers. God's kingdom does not recognize geographical, social or any other kind of boundaries which may make a difference in the rights and duties between one human being and another.

We have to recognize, though, with grief and contrition, that much of the trouble and confusion in the world, its warlike, competitive and unbalanced conditions we owe to the much divided church, which for a long time engaged in internal strife, in fruitless polemics of doctrinal or ecclesiastical matters, alienated from the world and its grave problems. Fortunately the Holy Spirit is making the church aware of the reality of its situation, exhorting it to assemble in unity, to seek to be the instrument for the salvation of the world. All of humanity cannot be united if the Christian church is divided or interested only in saving itself. In this state of disunion and isolation it will neither be saved nor save the world. It has to hear again, on its knees, our Lord's prayer:

> *As thou didst send me into the world, so I have sent*
> *them into the world. And for their sake I consecrate*
> *myself, that they also may be consecrated in truth. I*

*do not pray for these only, but also for those who
believe in me through their word, that they may all be
one; even as thou, Father, art in me, and I in thee,
that they also may be in us, so that the world may
believe that thou hast sent me.*
—John 17:18-21

To pray on its knees, yes; and then get up conscious that it is
bound to answer affirmatively this prayer of its master, and carry
out the mission with which it was entrusted, marching as an
obedient servant of a Lord who "came not to be served but to
serve, and to give his life as a ransom for many" (Mark 10:45).
Only then can we hope to see humankind united as one family
and men at home in any place on the earth.

Jesus is calling us today to be part of a world citizenship. He
calls us urgently, before it is too late and because this is the only
hope of salvation for humanity. We have, therefore, to make
efforts toward integrating the whole human race, in the common
vocation of Christ, which is the vocation of life. The responsibil-
ity of the Christian church is tremendous. We have to summon
the young people and give them a place so that they may feel
challenged by this kingdom of Jesus, so that they may dedicate
themselves to struggle against all oppressive force, be it military
or civil, against all intolerance, lack of cooperation, exploitation
of man by man, hate, poverty, discrimination.

When I found myself, during my life a pilgrim in the world—a
pilgrim even before being born, in my mother's womb—I felt my
national orphanhood and when people called me *a foreigner,* I
felt it even more deeply. I found, though, in Jesus, my world
brother; and I found in his kingdom my citizenship, which no-
body can take from me. Today I no longer feel a stranger any-
where, in the midst of any people, because the whole earth is
God's earth, and all people have their origin in God, because
Christ gave me a dimension of life which does not know geo-
graphical limits, and gave me a humanistic vision with which to
see every man and woman as my companion towards eternity. I
give thanks to God for his infinite grace.

The Challenge of the Communication of the Gospel
The Unavoidable Mission of Christians

ACCORDING to the book of the Apostles, the last recommendation of Jesus given to his closest disciples was: "You shall receive power when the Holy Spirit has come upon you; and you shall be my witnesses in Jerusalem and in all Judea and Samaria and to the end of the earth" (Acts 1:8). Those instructions, given in such brief words, sum up a whole program of activities which would project itself through time and space. It was a plan which had its beginning in the person and in the mission of that very speaker. The carpenter of Galilee was enlarging, in this way, the scope of his Palestinian task into one of unforeseen dimensions.

He was about to leave the visible scene for an invisible one, though he would never be too far away, since his promise had been: "Lo, I am with you always, to the close of the age" (Matt. 28:20).

He was not, then, withdrawing from his mission: he would continue to carry it out, but from another perspective and dimension. In one of his visits to the historic Upper Room, after his resurrection, he declared: "As the Father has sent me, even so I send you" (John 20:21). He was sending them, but not in their own power, but in the power of his spirit, who, in them, would be their dynamics, as expressed by the apostle Paul in his Roman prison: "I can do all things in him [Christ] who strengthens me" (literally who is dynamizing me) (Phil. 4:13). The disciples could continue his ministry only if they were conscious recipients of his integrating and inspiring spirit.

Who were those who received such an extraordinary recommendation? They were the same rustic men who, from Galilee, had followed him to the capital city of Judea, Jerusalem. They had abandoned everything—boats, custom-houses, and other trades—to go with him.

They had not received fine schooling—except the tutoring they got in their wandering journeys with Jesus, through their native country. They did not have earthly belongings, political influence, or economic power. They had only the promise of becoming citizens of a kingdom, which was to come, and that they hoped would soon be established from one end of the earth to the other. And because they really thought that time was already pressing near, they hastened to proclaim its coming; but Jesus had told them that they should not start, before God had given them the assurance that he would be with them to carry out the enterprise.

Truly, the book of the Acts of the Apostles is the chronicle of the action of the spirit of God "turning the world upside down" (Acts 17:6), through witnesses who apparently were very deficient and ridiculous. Certainly Paul must have referred to this fact when he wrote to the Corinthian brethren: "God chose what is low and despised in the world, even things that are not, to bring to nothing things that are, so that no human being might boast in the presence of God" (1 Cor. 1:28-29).

They were to be the light of a light which would shine on their spirits: to go throughout the world to retell the story of a man who had died on a cross, because he loved the world, that is, every human creature. It was the story of a man-carpenter, whom men wanted to criminally blot out, but whom God did elevate to be "Lord and Christ" (Acts 2:36), immortalizing him in his love; the history of a man who made himself poor so as to enrich the life of his brothers, to whom he promised "abundant life" (John 10:10) here, now and for the age of ages.

Jesus knew his disciples' limitatons, but he would convert himself into their sufficiency through the manifestation of his spirit. They, meanwhile, had the unavoidable responsibility of being his witnesses, and, as such, had to be always ready for the unexpected changes which could occur in the world. It is true that Jesus, during the time he was with them, taught them many things which would remain in their minds and consciences, but this was in a limited region of the earth and section of humanity. Now he was sending them out unto the whole earth and to the whole of humanity and thus, they would be subjected to sudden and strange occurrences. Certainly it was for this very reason that he, on the night of his farewell, said: "I have yet many things to say to you, but you cannot bear them now. When the Spirit of truth comes, he will guide you into all the truth; for he will not speak on his own authority, but whatever he hears he will speak, and he will declare to you the things that are to come. He will glorify me, for he will take what is mine and declare it to you" (John 16:12-14). There is no doubt that Jesus has still to direct us in many of the hidden truths of this world, where many unforeseen changes take place. In the same way that the Primitive Church was compelled to subject itself to the orders of the Spirit to start the mission of the kingdom of God, as its successor, we have to search continually for the orientation of the Spirit.

How does the Spirit manifest itself? It is certainly not limited by any frontier; neither is it locked up in some imaginary or concrete place. Truly it can speak to us through means which we frequently do not imagine. It can lead us to action through the Holy Scriptures. It can reveal itself through the cry of a child, the beauty of a flower, the flight of a bird, the pain of an agonizing being, the poverty of a hungry person, the desperation of a lost one, the injustice of a political or economic system, the alienation of an ambitious spirit.

"God is spirit" Jesus said to the Samaritan woman (John 4:24). He is the one who reveals himself everywhere and who "with sighs too deep for words" (Rom. 8:26) awakens our conscience so that we may discern what sometimes we do not want to see, and hear what we do not want to understand. Unhappily, we give him few opportunities to determine our conduct, because we trust our own wisdom or the convenience of the moment.

The apostle Paul, when he went to meet the Corinthians for the first time, said: "When I came to you, brethren, I did not come proclaiming to you the testimony of God in lofty words or wisdom. For I decided to know nothing among you except Jesus Christ and him crucified" (1 Cor. 2:1-2).

All his interest was focused on setting them face to face with Jesus, to present to them, first of all, his spirit of sacrifice; to show them the greatness of God's love manifested in him; to show them that God was not found in the power which decrees, or in intelligence which produces pride, or in greatness which corrupts, but in the simple and sacrificial life that leaves in its path, though unperceived, accomplishments conceived in response to the outrages perpetuated against human dignity.

We have to agree that Paul did not despise true wisdom, that which served divine truth, but did despise knowledge which transforms itself into vanity, presumption, opposition to wholesome virtue, and, which, arrogantly, puts itself on the throne of authority to degrade and destroy.

When Paul introduces Jesus Christ, he does it so that our profession of faith may not be, as he declares, a vain verbal manifestation of our intention to follow him; our human integration was not to be a question of words and incense, it would cost blood on Calvary and anguish of the spirit. For this reason, the Apostle gives the following warning to the Corinthians: "My speech and my message were not in plausible words of wisdom, but in demonstration of the Spirit and of power, that your faith might not rest in the wisdom of men but in the power of God" (1 Cor. 2:4-5).

And here, it is proper to ask if our Christian task, in the world which surrounds us, and faced with the tremendous problems which defy us, consists of "plausible words of wisdom" or in the "demonstration of the Spirit and power." At this point, it is well to remember the admonition of our teacher: "Not every one who says to me 'Lord, Lord,' shall enter the kingdom of heaven, but he who does the will of my Father who is in heaven." (Matt. 7:21).

It is certainly easier to raise altars and have Christ "seated at the right hand of God" than to go with him where he "has nowhere to lay his head" (Matt. 8:20), or discover his challenge in a suffering face, or in a corrupted soul. Truly, he did not come primarily to assert his person. His person is the revelation of God, and the interest of God is that man may become what he should be. Jesus is the link between the humanity of God, and the divinity of man. The humanity of God comes to us in Jesus Christ, so that he may disclose to us the possibility of divinity which exists in our humanity; in other words, he comes to transfer us from our animalism to the humanity of God. We should not forget, as we already intimated, that he said: "I came that they may have life, and have it abundantly" (John 10:10). When Jesus states that he came to bestow on us life, abundant life, he meant that he had come to make us citizens of an everlasting kingdom, which he designated as the "Kingdom of God" or "of heaven." This kingdom, according to Saint Paul, "is not food and drink but righteousness and peace and joy in the Holy Spirit" (Rom. 14:17). Man is not really man until, in the Holy Spirit, he acquires a sense of what is "justice and peace and joy."

On a certain occasion, the great Spanish thinker and philosopher Miguel de Unamuno, was asked what his religion was, and he answered: "My religion is to seek truth in life, and life in truth, even knowing that I shall not find it while I am still living; my religion is a ceaseless struggle with mystery; my religion is to strive with God from dawn till dusk, as they say that Jacob struggled. We are afraid of the eternal. In any case, I want to elevate myself to the unattainable. 'Be you perfect, as your Father in heaven is perfect,' Christ said to us, but such an ideal of perfection is beyond our reach. But he set before us the unattainable as the goal and end of our efforts. This happened—the theologians say—by grace. I want to fight the good fight, without being preoccupied with winning."

The kingdom of God is, therefore, in the first place, an inner good, and there is no external kingdom of God, if, first, it does not exist internally, just as an outward sign of Christ does not really exist, if he does not reveal himself inwardly, till we feel as Saint Paul did, when he stated to the Galatian brethren: "I have been crucified with Christ; it is no longer I who live, but Christ who lives in me; and the life I now live in the flesh I live by faith in the Son of God, who loved me and gave himself for me" (Gal. 2:20). In the same way that the reality of truth is not real until we feel it to be real in our inner being, so also moral evil cannot be measured only by its actions, but by its internal reality, by what moral putrefaction exists within the spirit. It was certainly for this reason that Jesus advised: "What comes out of a man is what defiles a man. For from within, out of the heart of man, come evil thoughts, fornication, theft, murder, adultery, coveting, wickedness, deceit, licentiousness, envy, slander, pride, foolishness. All these evil things come from within, and they defile a man'' (Mark 7:20-23).

Let us ask, therefore: where do we seek God's kingdom? It would be foolishness to seek it outside ourselves, here, there, yonder. If we do not feel it within us first, it will not be anywhere. Jesus did caution us: "The kingdom of God is not coming with signs to be observed; not will they say, 'Lo, here it is' or 'There!' for behold, the kingdom of God is in the midst of you'' (Luke 17:20-21).

The order given by Jesus indicates that we have to go "to the ends of the earth." What he is really saying is that his kingdom has no limits or frontiers, or, also, that it reaches any boundary just to tear it down. He said that the task should begin in Jerusalem, in Judea and Samaria and then go "to the ends of the earth." We could say that it starts within our being, village, city, county, state, till it reaches the boundaries of our country. However it does not end there. It extends itself throughout the whole terrestrial globe. Our frontiers may not be geographical—they may be very near us, in our own home, in our office, in our community, because anything which destroys human beings, and divides them, and exploits them, and loses them may be near us. "The ends of the earth," therefore, may not be in Africa, Oceania, or in some region of our America, but in our home or in the home of our neighbor. We may set up boundaries to our love. Reading some missionary book, we may feel in ourselves grief for the African in Rhodesia, or in the Union of South Africa, or for the natives of Haiti, but however, not feel the pain of those groaning, suffering, and lost in our quarter or slum, or of the natives in the jungles of our own country.

Let us inquire if in our own American continent there are not innumerable human beings who really do not know the crucified and resurrected Christ? Moreover, let us remember those who "hunger and thirst for righteousness," the many children who never attend school; the many who never satisfied their hunger, the many who died and will die in pain—without relief and consolation; the many who have faded or will fade away without having been able to really live; the many who are desperate and will never be conscious of their humanity. All this is summed up in the crucifixion of Jesus, in his suffering, in his word, in the permanent agony of his spirit.

John Wesley wrote to a young man full of evangelistic enthusiasm, who had offered to go as a missionary to the New World, where some Methodists from England had gone: "I let you loose, George, on the great continent of America. Publish your message in the open face of the sun and do all the good you can" (Letters, 1773). This is also our mandate: to announce openly our message under the sun's light—without boundaries. There, where human beings need orientation, help, consolation, justice, love, hope, assistance. Yes, under the sun's light—and under the inspiration of the Holy Spirit and in the immediate situation in which we find ourselves.

In reality our sun is Jesus Christ, who, like the physical sun, wants to illuminate fully every human creature in the whole world. This should be our passion, so that this may be accomplished. It needs to be an irresistible passion, like that of Saint Paul, when he wrote to the Corinthians: "Woe to me if I do not preach the gospel!" (1 Cor. 9:16). Let us remember that Christians have to be a pilgrim people. The commandment of Jesus is: "Go . . ." Therefore, they can never sit down at the edge of the road to watch those who pass by, rather they have to march in front of them to show them the way, the only way: CHRIST.

The Woman with Christ

Excerpt from the last of four messages given in the Congress of Methodist Women of Latin America, under the general title "The Woman with Christ" celebrated in Porto Alegre, Brazil, in March, 1981.

IT IS WELL to remember some of the last of Jesus' declarations after his resurrection: "As the Father has sent me, even so I send you" (John 20:21). "Go therefore and make disciples of all nations . . . and lo, I am with you always, to the close of the age" (Matt. 28:19-20). "You shall receive power when the Holy Spirit has come upon you; and you shall be my witnesses in Jerusalem, and in all Judea and Samaria and to the end of the earth" (Acts 1:8).

In connection with these words of Jesus Christ we should notice two things:

a. the promise of his presence and cooperation;

b. The mandate to go, from the place where we find ourselves, to "the end of the earth," and to convert all nations, preaching and teaching all the things which he taught through his preaching, teaching and life.

a. That he has been with us, for almost twenty centuries, is proven by the existence of the Christian community throughout the world. According to his own statement, without his presence, it could not have subsisted: ". . . apart from me you can do nothing" (John 15:5). He, as Saint Paul states, ". . . is the head of the church, his body, and is himself its Savior" (Eph. 5:23). This statement is the affirmation of the former: without a head, the body is dead. We should never forget this fact: Christ is the living Spirit who energizes the Church, which is (or should be) his visible presence in the world.

b. The world, that is, humanity, is far from having been evangelized. Our American reality gives testimony of this, even if we do not consider the rest of the world, which really is less evangelized than our section of it. The commandment *to go* is still as valid as it was when first given by him, or perhaps more so now, because the world's population is growing tremendously. Our mandate is never to rest. God's love should compel us to be always on the move. Jesus does not say that we should wait for people to come to us: we should go to find them as Jesus "went about doing good and healing all that were oppressed by the devil" (Acts 10:38). We may ask: how will we find Christ and where should we start and end? There is no fixed boundary; wherever a human need is detected: physical, moral, spiritual, there the disciple of Christ should be found. That human need is the voice of Christ, calling at the door of our conscience: "I stand at the door and knock" (Rev. 3:20). And if we open, he will say " 'Truly, I say to you, as you did it to one of the least of these my brethren, you did it to me' " (Matt. 25:40).

And who are these "least of my brethren." The hungry, the thirsty, the homeless, the lost, the ragged, the prisoner, the sick, the forgotten, those lost in vices and sin, the violent, the envious, the tyrant. All of them in some way are lost people, void of love, subject to pain or passion, all of them under God's grace. We all are "God's fellow workers" (1 Cor. 3:9), sent by Christ.

The task is not easy, it was never easy, except for those who seek to secure their salvation "on Christ's merits," and who do not advance from there, but only wait for the day of their death, hoping to be sent to heaven. But for the true disciple of Christ the mandate is: "Take up [your] cross and follow me" (Mark 8:34). This cross is the call for an integral testimony, through proclamation and action. The task is every day more complex, and, therefore, more urgent and necessary, requiring more daring and fidelity.

Evidently, we have to first meet the human needs of persons who are closest to us, without waiting for the day when the social structures will be changed, because we do not know for sure when this will come about. In any social condition in which we may find ourselves, our most urgent duty is to assist the fellow being closest to us who is lost or suffering.

There are tasks for the individual person and for the group. In a group the apostolic women went, serving the Christian Church in its genesis, through Christ and his apostles (Luke 8:1-3). They remained together, when the apostles and other disciples met in the Upper Room. There they were when on the day of Pentecost, the Holy Spirit manifested itself, according to the saying of Saint Peter, to "all flesh," "sons and daughters," "young men . . . and old men," "menservants and maidservants" (Acts 2:17-21).

Here the universality of the manifestation of the Holy Spirit is underscored. There is no man or woman: there are men and women of every condition and age. And in this way, you Methodist women of Latin America are here now, as if you were in the Upper Room in Jerusalem, waiting again for the call of God in the Holy Spirit.

As I was saying, the task is enormous. It is as great on the personal as it is on the group level of women's activities. Concerning the group level, Christian women must stand beside the men's group; they must travel together the paths of America, as the apostolic women accompanied Christ and his apostles from Galilee to Jerusalem and beyond.

The program of human salvation, till it attains a substantial change in social structure, is enormous, but without the decisive, frank, heroic support of the women, it will not reach its climax.

It is necessary to face new, enormous obstacles, but nothing is impossible for those who have faith in God, and in the assistance of the Holy Spirit.